ESSENTIALS OF
Interpretative Phenomenological Analysis

Essentials of Qualitative Methods Series

ESSENTIALS OF

Interpretative Phenomenological Analysis

Jonathan A. Smith
Isabella E. Nizza

 AMERICAN PSYCHOLOGICAL ASSOCIATION

The opinions and statements published are the responsibility of the authors, and such opinions and statements do not necessarily represent the policies of the American Psychological Association.

Published by
American Psychological Association
750 First Street, NE
Washington, DC 20002
https://www.apa.org

Order Department
https://www.apa.org/pubs/books
order@apa.org

In the U.K., Europe, Africa, and the Middle East, copies may be ordered from Eurospan
https://www.eurospanbookstore.com/apa
info@eurospangroup.com

Typeset in Charter and Interstate by Circle Graphics, Inc., Reisterstown, MD

Printer: Gasch Printing, Odenton, MD
Cover Designer: Anne C. Kerns, Anne Likes Red, Inc., Silver Spring, MD

Library of Congress Cataloging-in-Publication Data

Names: Smith, Jonathan A., author. | Nizza, Isabella E., author.
Title: Essentials of interpretative phenomenological analysis / by Jonathan A. Smith
  and Isabella E. Nizza.
Description: Washington, DC : American Psychological Association, [2022] |
  Series: Essentials of qualitative methods series | Includes bibliographical
  references and index.
Identifiers: LCCN 2021008085 (print) | LCCN 2021008086 (ebook) |
  ISBN 9781433835650 (paperback) | ISBN 9781433835681 (ebook)
Subjects: LCSH: Phenomenological psychology. | Psychology—Research—Methodology.
Classification: LCC BF204.5.S57 2022 (print) | LCC BF204.5 (ebook) |
  DDC 150.19/2—dc23
LC record available at https://lccn.loc.gov/2021008085
LC ebook record available at https://lccn.loc.gov/2021008086

https://doi.org/10.1037/0000259-000

Printed in the United States of America

10 9 8 7 6 5

Contents

Series Foreword

Qualitative approaches have become accepted and indeed embraced as empirical methods within the social sciences, as scholars have realized that many of the phenomena in which we are interested are complex and require deep inner reflection and equally penetrating examination. Quantitative approaches often cannot capture such phenomena well through their standard methods (e.g., self-report measures), so qualitative designs using interviews and other in-depth data-gathering procedures offer exciting, nimble, and useful research approaches.

Indeed, the number and variety of qualitative approaches that have been developed is remarkable. We remember Bill Stiles saying (quoting Chairman Mao) at one meeting about methods, "Let a hundred flowers bloom," indicating that there are many appropriate methods for addressing research questions. In this series, we celebrate this diversity (hence, the cover design of flowers).

The question for many of us, though, has been how to decide among approaches and how to learn the different methods. Many prior descriptions of the various qualitative methods have not provided clear enough descriptions of the methods, making it difficult for novice researchers to learn how to use them. Thus, those interested in learning about and pursuing qualitative research need crisp and thorough descriptions of these approaches, with lots of examples to illustrate the method so that readers can grasp how to use the methods.

The purpose of this series of books, then, is to present a range of qualitative approaches that seemed most exciting and illustrative of the range of methods appropriate for social science research. We asked leading experts in qualitative methods to contribute to the series, and we were delighted that they accepted our invitation. Through this series, readers have the opportunity to learn qualitative research methods from those who developed the methods and/or who have been using them successfully for years.

We asked the authors of each book to provide context for the method, including a rationale, situating the method within the qualitative tradition, describing the method's philosophical and epistemological background, and noting the key features of the method. We then asked them to describe in detail the steps of the method, including the research team, sampling, biases and expectations, data collection, data analysis, and variations on the method. We also asked authors to provide tips for the research process and for writing a manuscript emerging from a study that used the method. Finally, we asked authors to reflect on the methodological integrity of the approach, along with the benefits and limitations of the particular method.

This series of books can be used in several different ways. Instructors teaching courses in qualitative research could use the whole series, presenting one method at a time to expose students to a range of qualitative methods. Alternatively, instructors could choose to focus on just a few approaches, as depicted in specific books, supplementing the books with examples from studies that have been published using the approaches, and providing experiential exercises to help students get started using the approaches.

In this volume, Smith and Nizza provide clear descriptions, with many examples, of how to conduct interpretative phenomenological analysis (IPA), a method based on the philosophical foundations of phenomenology, hermeneutics, and idiography. IPA researchers focus on lived experiences and how people make sense of these experiences within the context of their personal and social worlds. IPA goes beyond summaries of what people have said to trying to make sense of what the experience is like from the person's view. Rather than being prescriptive about exact steps that must be followed, they provide an engaging and encouraging framework appropriate for both beginners and professionals who want to learn how to conduct IPA.

—*Clara E. Hill and Sarah Knox*

ESSENTIALS OF

Interpretative Phenomenological Analysis

1 WHAT IS INTERPRETATIVE PHENOMENOLOGICAL ANALYSIS?

Imagine waking up on your first day at university away from home: You open your eyes and look around your new room; it is a sunny day, so you set out to explore the campus. You have been looking forward to starting university for a long time. You arrived late last night; it was dark, and you went straight to your room, so this is your first day as a university student.

So, what is that like? What is it like in the moment to realize that this is the start of a new time for you? Can you describe that feeling? What is it doing to you physically? What thoughts come to mind? How does it relate to what you expected? Now describe your walk around campus, looking at the buildings, working out how to find the library, eating at the cafeteria, watching other students and academics, talking to some of them. The experience of your first day at university is an example of a topic suitable to be investigated using interpretative phenomenological analysis (IPA).

IPA is a method designed to understand people's lived experience and how they make sense of it in the context of their personal and social worlds (Smith et al., 2009). IPA can be used to address a variety of research questions in different areas. For example, there are published IPA studies exploring major life changes, such as becoming a parent or migrating; health-related

https://doi.org/10.1037/0000259-001
Essentials of Interpretative Phenomenological Analysis, by J. A. Smith and I. E. Nizza

experiences, such as receiving a medical diagnosis or living with a chronic illness; mental health issues, such as living with depression or recovering from psychosis; emotional experiences, such as feelings of wonder or awe, anger or guilt; professional experiences, such as being a therapist or a health care worker; and issues of identity, such as being a musician or being homeless. While early IPA studies were primarily in psychology, the approach has now been adopted in many disciplines to address many research questions, and IPA research is conducted in many different countries in the world.

With IPA, the objective is to get as close as possible to the lived experience of participants so that it can be examined in detail. Accordingly, IPA researchers aim for insight into what it is like to have an experience from the point of view of the person who has had it to elicit rich descriptions, trying to capture the emotions surrounding the experience and how people understand it and make sense of it. The personal meanings associated with lived experience are considered particularly important in IPA, as is how the experience relates to people's views of their world and their relationships.

So, what do we gain from an IPA study? First and foremost, it gives an opportunity to get a close and detailed understanding of what an experience has been like for an individual and how they make sense of it. IPA is particularly valuable when those experiences are of great importance to participants. The approach is also especially good at illuminating ambiguity and tensions in people's reactions to what is happening to them. IPA studies can stand on their own as detailed academic accounts of lived experience. They can also help illuminate prior quantitative studies by providing rich and nuanced analyses of constructs of interest. IPA work can also be drawn on by practitioners to assist with designing and making sense of their interactions and interventions with clients.

IPA is one of a number of different qualitative methods now used in psychology. While psychology has traditionally been dominated by quantitative research methods, we are witnessing a fast-growing recognition of the added value that qualitative approaches can bring to research. Quantitative and qualitative approaches to research are complementary, offering answers to different research questions and providing an understanding of the human mind in different ways. Where quantitative studies are generally hypothesis driven and based on a quantification of the phenomena under study so that statistical methods can be applied, most qualitative studies are used to answer open exploratory questions, and researchers tend to engage with linguistic descriptions of the phenomena they study and analyze them textually.

This is an exciting time for those of us who are interested in qualitative research, as qualitative methods are included in many undergraduate and postgraduate curricula, and a growing number of students are choosing to carry out qualitative research projects. The recent American Psychological Association (APA)–sponsored publication guidelines (Levitt et al., 2018) reflect an expanding interest in qualitative research in the United States.

The publication by the APA of the series of which this book is a part is indicative of how qualitative research is not a single entity but rather a collection of approaches, each with its own defining methodological features and theoretical underpinnings. In this book, we introduce you to IPA, explore its origins, and provide practical guidance on how to use it, assuming you have limited or no experience with qualitative methods. To make the topic more approachable, we provide examples using data from our published and unpublished studies. While IPA originated in psychology, it is now used by researchers in many subject areas. Hence, we are writing this book for anyone interested in learning more about the methodology, regardless of disciplinary background.

Because different qualitative methods are defined by their own set of philosophical underpinnings, we start by providing you with an overview of the ideas and theories on which IPA draws and explain the purpose of some of IPA's distinguishing characteristics. Then, step by step, we guide you through the stages of an IPA project. Our primary aim is for this book to provide practical guidance to students and researchers approaching IPA for the first time. At the end, you will find a list of the references cited throughout the book, including methodological articles, chapters, and books on IPA, and there is an appendix giving examples of good IPA studies you might find useful.

A NOTE ON TERMINOLOGY

In this book, we introduce some modifications to the terminology employed in doing IPA. This is a result of an exercise with two other senior figures in IPA: Paul Flowers and Michael Larkin, who, along with Jonathan Smith, wrote the first book on IPA in 2009 (Smith et al., 2009). The new book you are now reading was written at the same time as a second edition of the older book is being prepared. The two books are complementary. This book is a short introductory text; the other book is a fuller and more advanced volume. In preparing the two books, we have all considered how the procedures for doing IPA are described. We think most of it works well, but we have decided to modify a small number of the terms used in describing the analytic process to make them clearer. We use the new terms in the chapter on analysis and describe the changes we have made in a footnote at the relevant point. We are confident readers will find the new terminology helpful.

We use the full original spelling for interpretative phenomenological analysis in this book. Readers may sometimes come across an alternative spelling for the same approach: interpretive phenomenological analysis.

THEORETICAL UNDERPINNINGS OF IPA

A helpful way of understanding the different qualitative approaches is to subdivide them into two large categories: experiential and discursive (Reicher, 2000). As the name suggests, *experiential* methods are commonly used to explore human experience from the point of view of those who are having the experience. Participants are considered experiential experts in the topic under investigation, so their input is obtained to understand what has happened to them or to know what their thoughts and feelings on a certain topic are. The focus is on what they do (or have done), think, and feel about the experience. Although researchers have different standpoints in the value they assign to participants' accounts (e.g., whether they consider the accounts to be a reflection of objective reality or a subjective interpretation of it), the focus with experiential approaches is mostly on the contents of the accounts that participants provide. *Discursive* methods, however, stem from a strongly social constructionist view of the world (Burr, 2006), and researchers using them are primarily interested in how we, as people, talk about ourselves and the world around us. The focus is on language as the means through which reality is coconstructed, and the aim is to understand how language is used to create meaning. For example, an experiential researcher and a discursive researcher may both interview a person with a heart condition. The experiential researcher will draw on what the person says in the interview to make an interpretation of how the condition is impacting them and their life. The discursive researcher will be interested in the language that the person is able to draw on to give an account of being ill. For more on discursive analysis, see the relevant volume by McMullen (2021) in this book series.

As you may imagine from what we have said so far, IPA can be classified as an experiential method. More specifically, it has three primary theoretical underpinnings: phenomenology, hermeneutics, and idiography. We should clarify that IPA is not philosophy. It is an approach developed for the close examination of participants' experience. This approach draws on philosophical principles in the process of establishing a set of procedures and techniques to enable that examination and analysis of accounts of experience provided by those participants. What are privileged then are the research processes, but it is important that these are anchored in the theoretical ideas. We hope this connection between theory and practice is apparent throughout the book. It is important first, however, to give a short statement on the underlying theoretical ideas themselves.

Phenomenology is a philosophical approach to the study of human experience. A founding principle of phenomenological inquiry is that experience should be examined in the way it occurs and on its own terms, rather than according to predefined theoretical categories (Ashworth, 2015). Husserl (1859–1938) was the first phenomenological philosopher to write programmatically about this approach. He wanted to understand how the experience of a given phenomenon could be known accurately enough to determine its essential qualities. Husserl (1900/2001) is famously quoted as asserting the need to "go back to the things themselves" (p. 168), by which he meant the core components of our consciousness. Husserl was critical of the claims by his contemporary scientists to a privileged access to knowledge. He thought our everyday life, or lifeworld, should provide the grounding for objective scientific work, so a study of subjective experience should be the precursor for any subsequent scientific account of the world. Similarly, when conducting phenomenological inquiry, we should strive to put aside existing scientific constructs or any presupposed view of the world, which can act as a concealing barrier from the experience under investigation, to focus on our own perception of the world. The focus on examining lived experience through one's conscious awareness and reflection are central to most phenomenological methods of inquiry, including IPA.

Heidegger (1889–1976) was a student of Husserl's who inherited his tutor's commitment to a close examination of experience in its own terms. However, Heidegger's phenomenology took on its own distinctive qualities. Heidegger (1927/1962) emphasized the worldly nature of our subjective experience as we engage in our daily practical activities. He also added a temporal dimension to phenomenology and, in particular, was concerned with the individual life as something finite, which had mortality.

Heidegger was also influenced by *hermeneutics*, which is the theory of interpretation. Crucially, from an IPA perspective, he articulated the importance of viewing phenomenology as an interpretative endeavor. Heidegger considered that the meaning of experience was not always self-evidently visible and that getting at that meaning involved digging deeper beyond the surface appearance or account. Therefore, being phenomenological involves detective work, closely engaging with what is seen or said, searching for clues to work out what it actually means.

IPA researchers recognize that it is not just the researcher who is interpretative but also the participant. People generally do not just passively receive big things that happen in their lives: They try to make sense of them. In IPA, we talk about research involving a *double hermeneutic* (Smith & Osborn, 2003, p. 51) whereby the participant is trying to make sense of what is happening to them while the researcher is trying to make sense of the participant's sense making.

The final major theoretical perspective influencing IPA is idiography. *Idiography* is defined as a focus on the particular and is often discussed in contrast to a *nomothetic* approach, which is concerned with establishing laws or generalizations that can be valid for a population of people. Quantitative researchers normally adopt a nomothetic approach by testing hypotheses and formulating theories that aim to say something about the whole group under question. The problem with such an approach is that even though data may have been collected from a particular person in the first place, the process of analysis moves away from being able to say distinctive things about that person. Rather, findings are expressed in actuarial and probabilistic terms; so, for instance, a questionnaire designed to measure a psychological construct will indicate a certain probability of an individual displaying a given trait (Lamiell, 1987).

An alternative approach is the idiographic approach, in which the lens is focused closely on the case study. Here, by considering a single individual at a time, it is possible to examine their account in detail, in its own context and on its own terms. Social scientists have been slow in recognizing the value of an idiographic approach, which is surprising considering the insight it can afford on how meaning making occurs (Smith et al., 1995). Single cases can be intrinsically interesting and reveal factors that would be neglected in a group. Multiple cases can be compared to reveal which factors are similar and different across cases (Platt, 1988), and case studies can be combined to identify patterns, similar to what occurs in the development of case law (Bromley, 1986).

IPA is a strongly idiographic approach: There is an interest in understanding particular experiences of particular people in particular circumstances and a belief that this is best achieved by focusing on single cases to be analyzed individually before possibly making comparisons between cases. A move toward more generalized statements can still occur and, of course, often exists in IPA studies, but the move is made more cautiously. Good IPA studies of this type end up describing a pattern of convergence in the accounts provided by participants, but this is closely accompanied by an analysis of the particular and different ways participants express that commonality. And this process always involves linking general statements to specific instances by explicitly grounding statements in the data (Smith et al., 2009).

Thus, the objectives of IPA researchers are to collect detailed accounts about their experience from participants, extract the deepest meanings ascribed to those experiences through a case-by-case analysis, and convey them in a resonant manner to readers. These objectives determine the key features of IPA and are directly linked to its philosophical underpinnings:

- IPA researchers' interest in experience is influenced by the phenomenological tradition. There is a search for first-person subjective accounts of specific embodied life experiences. Most studies use in-depth interviews to obtain such accounts, so interviewing is an important skill for IPA researchers to have, although diaries, drawings, and other types of data are being increasingly used.

- The focus on meaning making of IPA researchers is influenced by the hermeneutic tradition. Accordingly, IPA interviewers often dwell on how participants make sense of their experience, and the analytical process is interpretative, with the analyst attempting to make sense of participants' sense making.

- The approach to the analysis when using IPA is case by case, making it an idiographic method. Each individual's experience is analyzed within the context of that individual's narrative before being compared with the experience of others or being considered in relation to theoretical models.

If you are interested in reading more about the theoretical underpinnings of IPA, we recommend the following papers: Smith (1996, 2007, 2019), Larkin et al. (2011), and Larkin et al. (2006).

IPA is one of a number of phenomenologically oriented qualitative approaches in contemporary human sciences. It is important first and foremost to emphasize what these different approaches have in common: They are all concerned with attempting to understand and document participants' lived experience, and they all wish to enable that experience to be expressed as far as possible in its own terms.

Beyond that, there are some differences in what a particular methodology emphasizes or how it is conducted. For example, IPA can be distinguished from another well-known phenomenologically oriented qualitative method developed in psychology: Giorgi's empirical phenomenological method. Giorgi (1997) attempted to produce a method that remains as close as possible to the principles of Husserl. Giorgi stated that it is a descriptive method that aims to produce the essence of experience—the general structure underlying different people's experience of a phenomenon. As we have seen with IPA, by contrast, phenomenology is conceived as a hermeneutic endeavor involving interpretation on the part of the participant and the researcher, and IPA researchers are concerned with retaining as far as possible the individual's experience. Rather than aiming to produce a single summary of the group experience, an IPA researcher attempts, through the idiographic, case-by-case process, to produce an analytic account that shows a patterning of convergence and differentiation in participants' experience of a similar phenomenon. The reader who is interested in more detail on other related phenomenological approaches is directed to the volume on existential phenomenological research by Churchill (2022) in this book series, Halling's (2008) dialogical phenomenology, Van Manen's (2016) hermeneutic phenomenology, Finlay's (2009) relational approach, and Todres et al.'s (2007) lifeworld approach.

As will become evident in the coming chapters, although IPA is not a particularly prescriptive method, its key features are determinant and jointly contribute to making IPA what it is, profoundly influencing how IPA is done. Let us now turn to the practicalities of doing IPA. In the next chapter, we consider what is involved in designing an IPA study.

2 DESIGNING AN IPA STUDY

The starting point for designing an interpretative phenomenological analysis (IPA) study is deciding what experience you want to investigate, who would be able to tell you about it, and the best way to obtain their account. These three factors go hand in hand and influence each other, so while there is a need to identify a research topic that is relevant and feasible, defining a topic will imply identifying participants who are able and willing to participate and will also imply choosing a data-gathering approach that will enable participants and researchers to provide the most insight into the phenomenon. The perfect balance will also consider the time frame and budget limitations of the study. Therefore, designing an IPA study requires combining what IPA can achieve theoretically with pragmatic considerations. In this chapter, each of these aspects is described in turn, though in reality, they occur in parallel and iteratively.

https://doi.org/10.1037/0000259-002
Essentials of Interpretative Phenomenological Analysis, by J. A. Smith and I. E. Nizza

CHOOSING A TOPIC AND A RESEARCH QUESTION

The primary aim of IPA researchers is to explore personal lived experience and how people think and/or feel about specific events that have happened to them or about processes in which they have been involved (the phenomena). IPA researchers aim to gather rich, detailed accounts from people about those experiences and then describe, interpret, and convey what the experience was like and how people made sense of it (Smith et al., 2009).

IPA could potentially be used to investigate any experience; however, the depth of understanding it enables makes it particularly suited to explore experiences that are perceived as highly significant. For instance, many published studies concern going through key life stages, such as becoming a mother, starting a new job, or retiring. Others examine living with or being diagnosed with a highly disabling physical or mental health condition.

Before you start your project, it is also a good idea to read some IPA papers, ideally on topics related to or similar to the area you are considering, to have a sense of the type of question you might ask, the type of insight you could achieve, and how the insight might be conveyed. See the Appendix for a list of good IPA papers.

IPA is not a theory-driven method but an inductive one, so conclusions are based on what is found in the data rather than on testing existing theories, as is the case for deductive reasoning. There is an argument for being naive to the topic you are investigating as a way of limiting your preconceptions and ensuring that you see participants as the topic "experts" rather than overimposing your own views or theories. However, a researcher who is too naive may find it difficult to understand the context of the participant and may miss asking important questions or end up reinventing the wheel. Therefore, some prior knowledge can be helpful. The literature search helps to attune you to work that has been done before. Looking closely at existing qualitative and quantitative studies and highlighting their strengths and limitations helps one to be clearer about what exactly one is interested in finding out and helps refine the research question. It is often the case that existing research offers an entrée to a topic that could be further illuminated by an intensive examination of individuals' personal experience of it—the rationale for an IPA study. The scale and extent of the literature search and review required vary by program and level of study.

Some IPA researchers are "insiders," meaning they share some aspects of the experience they are investigating, which has pros and cons. Being an insider means you have some awareness of the likely terrain of the conversations you will have. It might help with recruitment (by giving access to a specific group) and will mean you have a clear sense of who you will be talking to, thereby facilitating rapport. However, insiders may have strong and personal ideas about the experience, so an effort will be needed to put those aside when entering the phenomenological world of participants during an interview.

One useful exercise is to write a personal statement in the early stages of the study before you begin collecting any data. Here you record your current thoughts and beliefs about the topic under investigation. If you have personal experience of the phenomenon being researched, imagine how you might answer the questions of an investigator and summarize your possible responses in this account. Being explicit about your perceptions may help you bracket these as you conduct your interviews with participants. You may also want to refer back to it at various points as the research unfolds. If you are interested in reading more on these aspects of the role of the researcher during the research process, we point you to the more detailed book on IPA by Smith et al. (2009) that discusses it more fully.

Good IPA research questions focus on a specific contextualized experience, and they are open and exploratory (Smith et al., 2009). The aim is to gather participants' perceptions and sense making about the experience, be this a process or an end result, but not to reach conclusions in terms of cause and effect. Research questions are often worded using terms such as "exploring" or "investigating," reflecting IPA's inductive approach and its focus on meaning making and interpretation. See Exhibit 2.1 for some examples of research questions in published IPA studies.

DETERMINING WHAT TYPE OF DATA TO COLLECT

The important thing for an IPA study is to collect data that offers a rich and detailed insight into the participant's experience. A wide range of methods allows this: interviews, diaries, personal accounts, preexisting autobiographical accounts. As mentioned in Chapter 1, in-depth interviews are generally considered the most suitable source of data for IPA because of the

EXHIBIT 2.1. Examples of Research Questions Extrapolated From Published Studies

- What is professional dancers' experience of flow like? (Hefferon & Ollis, 2006)
- How do young people, foster parents, and social workers make sense of unplanned endings to foster placements? (Rostill-Brookes et al., 2011)
- How do participants experience dragon-boat races as an intervention for breast cancer survivors? (McDonough et al., 2011)
- What is it like for a woman to go through the transition to motherhood? (Smith, 1999)

opportunity they afford to gather the rich, first-person accounts of a phenomenon required for IPA. They are also, by far, the most commonly used data collection method in IPA. Therefore, for most of this book, we concentrate on in-depth interviews as the exemplary way of obtaining data for an IPA study.

The definition of what constitutes "rich data" is, of course, subjective, but during interviews, participants are generally able to answer questions freely, be reflective, and discuss their experiences at a good level of depth. The interview context also enables the interviewer to probe interactively for more information when needed (the next chapter contains a detailed description of the types of questions and prompts used during in-depth IPA interviews).

The aim of an in-depth interview is to obtain a full and deep level of disclosure that typically can be best achieved when interviewing in person—so far, the default approach for IPA. Recent years have seen an increase in audio or video-based remote interviewing. Although creating a good rapport can be more difficult remotely, this approach can be useful when meeting in person is not an option (e.g., because researcher or participant are unable to travel) or when the topic is so sensitive that the potential barrier created by the medium can occasionally actually become a facilitator (e.g., if the research topic is particularly embarrassing). However, virtual interviewing raises additional ethical concerns regarding the ability to show a duty of care to the participant at a distance. Ethical considerations are discussed later in this chapter.

SAMPLING AND RECRUITING PARTICIPANTS

The aim of IPA studies is to illuminate individual lived experience. This aim is achieved through purposive sampling (by choosing participants because they can provide insight into the specific experience being investigated). To achieve the optimal level of depth and understanding, IPA researchers have an idiographic commitment: Their analysis of each participant's account is done separately and in great detail, which takes time, so sample sizes tend to be small. Also, the focus on a specific experience calls for a homogenous sample: Participants need to be more ostensibly similar than they are ostensibly diverse so that differences between them are more likely to be accounted for by individual characteristics than by, for example, demographic characteristics. The overall sampling strategy is to identify a closely defined set of people for whom the experience has been particularly meaningful (Smith et al., 2009).

What would be classed as a homogenous sample depends on the circumstances. Imagine the variability you would be faced with if you wanted to investigate the experience of studying for undergraduate students in an American university and decided to recruit participants from all over the country. Their perspectives could differ according to whether they were young or mature students, what curriculum they were studying, at what institution they were studying, whether they were originally from the United States, whether they were working students, and so on. With a nonhomogenous sample, any differences emerging from analyzing the interviews could be due to any of these factors. If instead, you limited your sample to, for example, U.S.-born female students, aged 19 to 21, who are studying for a biology degree at a specific university and are not working while they study, any similarities or differences between them are likely to tell you something more about how that specific phenomenon is experienced by particular individuals. The results would also offer a deep understanding of what studying is like for the people in this specific group and, although you would need to be cautious in generalizing your findings to other groups, providing detailed information about the characteristics and context of your study would enable the reader to reflect on the degree of theoretical transferability by closely considering similarities and differences between the sample and context for your study and other situations they might encounter. Subsequent studies could also then look at a different group for fuller comparison and contrast.

At the same time, such considerations need to be pragmatically weighed against the actual availability of a sample. So, for instance, in a study about a rare disease, the number of potential participants could be so low that setting too many limits might affect feasibility. As a general rule, you should try to remain open to the possibility of reviewing sampling decisions as recruitment progresses. For instance, you might set out with tight recruitment criteria and then revisit them if finding participants proves to be particularly difficult.

Because the group of participants required is small and specific, recruitment tends to occur through referral by gatekeepers, by other participants (also known as *snowballing*), or through your own contacts. Sometimes recruitment is easy, but it can also be unexpectedly difficult, particularly in student projects on experiences that are not common and when there is time pressure to complete the work. Our advice is to think thoroughly about the recruitment strategy before committing to a project, but also be adaptable in modifying the focus of a study if recruitment proves tricky.

We have said IPA samples should be small, but how small? Even a single case study can yield rich and interesting results if the topic is complex and the data rich. Sample size also depends on the context of a project. For an undergraduate bachelor's project lasting a few months, our normal sample size is three participants. As you will become increasingly aware as you read this book, doing IPA is time-consuming and requires careful attention. A sample size of three allows a considerable amount of comparison across cases and gives the undergraduate sufficient data to master the main processes involved in doing IPA. A larger sample might lead to the student being overwhelmed and ending up only producing a mediocre analysis. We usually expect master's students to interview five participants for their study. Doctoral studies operate on a larger scale and can take a large variety of shapes and sizes and involve more sophisticated designs and/or analyses (see Chapter 7). It is, therefore, difficult to offer clear guidance on numbers. In general, if one is trying to publish an IPA study either as a doctoral student or postdoctoral researcher, 10 to 12 is a good number to aim for in one's sample.

PRACTICAL AND ETHICAL CONSIDERATIONS

So far, we have described IPA projects as time-consuming, but it might be helpful to understand why this is the case. Transcribing or checking a transcription, for example, can be surprisingly time-consuming. However, for both novice and experienced researchers, the analysis is where most of the effort will be invested. On the basis of our experience, a first-time researcher analyzing their first interview, from initial reading and exploratory noting to producing a complete analysis, may invest up to 3 weeks of full-time work. Subsequent interviews will probably be faster to analyze but will still require days, not hours. As will become clearer in Chapter 4, the analysis includes working closely with a transcript, often reviewing it word by word and multiple times, allowing for reflection and iteration, and sometimes discussing its contents with others. Once the individual cases have been analyzed, the comparison between cases will also require days of work. Finally, writing up an IPA analysis is a lengthy process because, as will become obvious in Chapter 5, the writing process is what gives the analysis its final shape. In our experience, students tend to underestimate the amount of time required for an in-depth analysis, possibly because they have only had experience with quantitative methods, where the analysis is usually not the most time-consuming task.

An IPA project is a long journey during which, particularly for the less experienced, it is important to be able to rely on the guidance and insight from somebody who is more experienced. Most student researchers will be working with an advisor or supervisor[1] who is experienced enough with IPA to provide methodological mentorship. If, however, your supervisor or advisor does not have specific working experience with IPA, we recommend you find another experienced IPA researcher who can act as your mentor during the project.

Researcher reflexivity implies being aware of our opinions and feelings in relation to the research in an attempt to monitor our influence on outcomes. It is an integral part of the research process, usually achieved by keeping a diary or research journal. When as a researcher you are an "insider" to the project topic, meaning that you share the experience that participants will be describing, being reflexive can be particularly challenging. In such cases, it can be helpful to put in writing your ideas and experience before you start the interviews; otherwise, your preconceptions could sneak in on you when you least expect them, causing you to ask a leading question or inadvertently express a judgment. A good way to become aware of your preconceptions is to ask a friend to interview you before you start interviewing others: There is nothing like talking about our experience to somebody else to discover how we really feel about it.

Ethical considerations are important in all research, and qualitative projects are no exception. Ethical research considerations normally aim to protect the people involved in the research and ensure that the research is carried out in a way that serves society, including issues such as risk, confidentiality, and informed consent. IPA researchers' aim to capture and analyze experience in depth means that some topics discussed in interviews and later analyzed can be sensitive and therefore unsettling for both participants and researchers. Informed consent processes are intended to safeguard participants and should be adhered to, not only before starting an interview but also during and after it. It is important to make clear to participants that they can refrain from answering questions that make them uncomfortable, interrupt the interview at any time, and withdraw their consent for their data to be used for a period after the interview has finished. At the end of each interview, it is good practice to assess how a participant is feeling. You may wish to direct the participant to someone who can offer guidance and advice. If, as can happen occasionally, the participant remains distressed, you should be able to discuss with them the possibility of their seeking psychological support. Finally, any identifying information (names, employers,

---

[1]*Advisor* and *supervisor* are equivalent terms. In the United States, the academic working with a student during their research project is generally called an *advisor*. In the United Kingdom, this person is described as the *supervisor*. Other countries may have other terms.

EXHIBIT 2.2. Traveling Solo at 18: A Case Study

This is a case study carried out for the purpose of this book. We wanted a topic that our readers could relate to, so we chose to examine the travel experience of a university student. Our research question was: What is it like to travel abroad on your own for the first time? We decided to gather our data through a single in-depth interview. We gained ethical approval from the relevant university ethics committee.

Our participant was Susan (a pseudonym), a 20-year-old British university student we recruited through a common acquaintance. Two years before the interview, after high school and before going to university, Susan took some time off to work and travel on her own in Southeast Asia for a few months.

Susan was interviewed on her own, and the interview lasted 75 minutes. She talked extensively, and at the end of the interview, she expressed surprise at how in depth her descriptions and considerations had been. Despite discussing some personal topics, Susan said she was not distressed by the interview. Therefore, there was no reason for us to consider discussing possible psychological support resources. For the moment, the study results have not been published in a journal.

and similar) must be anonymized using pseudonyms, and consent must explicitly extend to the publication of anonymized verbatim extracts from the data.

Researcher well-being (meaning their physical, emotional, and psychological welfare) is an aspect that is often overlooked but is important in IPA research for the level of depth with which researchers engage with their participants and the resulting data. Researchers are therefore advised to keep a reflexive journal, monitor their well-being during the course of the project, keep in close contact with their supervisor or advisor and, if in the unlikely event it becomes necessary, consider seeking professional psychological support.

Exhibit 2.2 describes the key design decisions relating to a small unpublished case study we conducted. Hopefully, it will help illuminate some of the issues discussed in this chapter. It is also the study that informs our presentation in Chapters 3 and 4.

Hopefully, you are now eager to learn more about how to conduct an IPA study. In the next chapters, we aim to guide you step by step through the various phases to collect, analyze, and report your data. Our tone is pretty didactic to help introduce IPA to novice researchers who may feel anxious anticipating the process. However, we also point to the degree of flexibility in IPA research. As you become more experienced, your IPA projects may become less linear and your methods more tailored to specific circumstances.

3 COLLECTING DATA

A prerequisite for good research is good data. With interpretative phenomenological analysis (IPA), this means rich and detailed first-person accounts of a specific experience. Participants need to be able to tell their story freely, on their own terms, taking the time to reflect and think about what to say, and to express their thoughts, feelings, and concerns without feeling judged. Your responsibility as a researcher is to create the environment that will enable the story to be told, listen carefully to your participants' narrative, and gently guide them so that their contribution can help answer your research question.

In-depth interviews are the most common way of gathering data for IPA analysis, and the ability to conduct a good in-depth interview is a fundamental skill for all IPA researchers.

IPA interviews are a particular form of conversation. The aim is for the interview to flow naturally and easily like a conversation, with the difference that the participant will do most of the talking while the researcher makes sure the conversation heads in a useful direction to gather the sought-after data. This is more easily said than done! Basic tools include developing an interview guide with the questions to be asked during the

https://doi.org/10.1037/0000259-003
Essentials of Interpretative Phenomenological Analysis, by J. A. Smith and I. E. Nizza

interview and an understanding of interviewing techniques, as we discuss in the next paragraphs. Our approach is a practical one, with examples mostly based on Susan's travel case study introduced in Exhibit 2.2 in the previous chapter.

RATIONALE FOR AN INTERVIEW GUIDE

Research questions are often formulated at an abstract and theoretical level in such a way that they cannot be posed directly to participants. Imagine taking part in a study in which you were asked straight on, "What impact has becoming a student had on your sense of identity?" Where would you start to answer such a question? Especially if you are not a social science student, a question like this could be confusing and daunting, and even if you were a psychologist, it might make you want to run away from the interview. Interview guides are a collection of simple, straightforward, open questions specifically ordered to gently steer participants toward responses that indirectly help us answer the study research question; in fact, the answer to the actual research question will probably become apparent only once the interview is fully analyzed. So, for example, a good interviewer might ask you questions such as "How did it happen that you chose your university?" and "How do you feel now that you are studying here?" and so on.

Having a good interview guide is important for a variety of reasons. First, to prepare the guide means to imagine the interview in great detail before it actually happens. It is an opportunity to design the questions and frame them appropriately, identify potentially sensitive topics and decide how best to tackle them, find the best wording for the most complex questions, and think of prompts that might help participants fully develop their responses. Having a guide also helps you feel prepared for the interview and more relaxed during the interview itself. Some participants will be talkative; others will be less forthcoming. Knowing the interview guide will help you manage difficult moments in the conversation because you will know what to ask next or how to encourage participants.

HOW TO DESIGN AN INTERVIEW GUIDE

The primary indicator of a good interview guide is how questions are worded: They should be open and expansive, using terms such as "how" and "what," to elicit answers that go beyond a yes or no. Assumptions should be avoided when wording questions so that participants are not directed toward giving a particular answer. In the example in Exhibit 3.1, most questions are open, and

EXHIBIT 3.1. Interview Guide for a Project on the Experience of Travel: Questions and Prompts

1. Question: Can you tell me how you decided to go on this journey?
   Prompts: Whose decision was it? Why there? Why then?

2. How did you prepare for the journey, if at all?
   How did you research it?

3. Did you have any expectations?
   What did you expect? What were your expectations based on?

4. What was your first impression when you got there?
   What struck you? How close was it to what you expected? In what way was it different?

5. What was it like afterward?
   What did you do? How did you feel?

6. What made the strongest overall impression on you?
   The people? The sights? The food? The climate? Why do you think you felt this way about it?

7. Tell me about something positive that happened while you were there.
   How did it make you feel? How does it feel now, thinking back?

8. Was there something difficult?
   What was it? How did it make you feel? How does it feel now, thinking back?

9. How did you keep in touch, if at all, with friends and family back home?
   How did they feel about you being away? How did you feel about being away from them?

10. What was it like to come back?
    How did you feel at the prospect? What was it like in practice?

11. What is the place of that experience in your life?
    Have you learned anything from it? Has it changed you as a person? Has it changed how you look at your life? Has it affected your desire to travel again?

Questions 3 and 8, despite being closed, are accompanied by open-worded prompts. We wanted to avoid assuming participants would have expectations (3) or that something difficult did happen during their journey (8).

Interview guides tend to include an alternation between questions that are descriptive and narrative and those that are more analytical and reflective. For instance, Question 1 in Exhibit 3.1 is descriptive because it is a factual question about what led to the decision to travel, whereas Question 2 is narrative because the answer requires thinking in temporal terms. With Question 3, the interview is becoming more reflective. Other types of questions include structural (where you ask participants to describe the steps involved in a certain process or the elements constituting a certain phenomenon), evaluative (such as Questions 6, 7, and 8 in the example, in which we were asking the participant to assess their experience), or circular (such as the prompts in Question 9, in which we asked how participants thought others felt about their travels).

A broad descriptive question concerning a specific experience or episode is always a good starting point: It helps break the ice and settles participants into the interview. The more complex and analytical questions are best kept for later on when rapport has been established and the participant is feeling comfortable and talking freely.

The best order for questions needs to be established. The earlier example follows a temporal structure: It starts from when the journey was being prepared, then continues with reaching the destination, asking about initial impressions first and concluding by retrospectively evaluating the experience. An alternative approach is the so-called funnel structure, in which initial topics are broad before questions become increasingly specific and more sensitive issues can be discussed (Brinkman & Kvale, 2015).

You may have noticed that in the example in Exhibit 3.1, most questions are followed by a set of prompts. These help to clarify the question and can be used on an as-needed basis. Although prompts should also be open questions, sometimes presenting a series of options can be helpful (see Question 6).

Probes, however, are not defined up-front; they are questions that emerge in the moment in response to something a participant has said, such as "Could you give me an example?" or "What do you mean when you say 'difficult'?" When during an interview we focus on what participants are saying and think in terms of depth and meaning making, probes come to mind quite spontaneously. Novice researchers may find it useful to consider using standard probes such as "Can you tell me a bit more about that?"

Some types of questions or ways of wording questions are best avoided. These include overemphatic questions (e.g., "That must have been terrible; what did you do?"), manipulative ones (e.g., "Did it get any worse?"), or leading ones (e.g., "Presumably, you say you were unhappy at that time?"). If the aim is to understand what the experience is like for participants, we need to be wary of making any suggestion that might influence how they describe it. Also to be avoided are double questions—single questions that are actually asking about two different things (e.g., "What were the best and worst things that happened to you?").

Preparing an interview guide takes time and is an iterative process. You should start by identifying the broad areas to be explored and then brainstorm possible questions and their order. Then, through multiple reviews, questions get refined, merged, broken down, or brought to a higher level. For a 45- to 60-minute interview, you should aim to have between six and 10 questions. Before using an interview guide, review it with an advisor or supervisor or a peer; it is surprising how somebody else can see what we have missed.

CONDUCTING THE INTERVIEW

Before conducting the actual data-gathering interview, it is advisable to speak personally with participants, maybe on the phone, so that you start to build a relationship and give them a sense of what to expect, in terms of interview duration and topics to be discussed.

The best place to interview someone is a quiet space, where you can both concentrate with no interruptions. When choosing a location, consider both the needs and preferences of participants and your safety. Many experienced IPA researchers interview people in their homes, but novice researchers may find it easier to concentrate in a private room at an academic institution. Unless the person being interviewed is vulnerable (e.g., a child), you should always aim to talk to them without anyone else being present.

You will need to audio-record the interview. You need a verbal record of everything said by the participant and the interviewer during the interview, and it is not possible to get this by attempting to write it all down while the interview is occurring. It is, of course, necessary to get permission from the participant to have the interview recorded, but we have never known a participant to refuse this.

It is good practice to memorize your guide before the interview because wondering what question should come next makes concentrating on what participants are saying difficult. Also, frequently looking at the guide while a participant is talking can be distracting for both of you and interrupt the flow. A good way to learn the guide and exercise your interviewing skills is to test it on a friend or a colleague who acts as a participant.

The guide is intended as a model for the researcher; however, during the interview, flexibility becomes paramount. It makes sense to start the interview with the first question in the guide. Once participants start talking, their answers may take you away from the guide; they may raise topics that you expected would be discussed later, or they may talk about something you had not considered at all. Having a good guide will give you the flexibility and confidence you need to focus on listening to what they are saying, probing for depth, following up on unexpected avenues while keeping track of what is being said and what still needs to be asked. So, although having a guide is important to prepare for the interview, ultimately, the interview needs to be a cooperative endeavor. When participants feel at ease and able to talk about what is important to them, their level of disclosure increases, making the data "richer" (Smith et al., 2009).

A good example of this dynamic occurred while interviewing Susan about her travels in the study we introduced at the end of the previous chapter. We designed the guide in Exhibit 3.1 to be open, although we expected that the most relevant aspects of the traveling experience would be related to the destination, as well as the culture and landmarks of the destination (e.g., see the prompts for Question 6). It became apparent fairly early in the interview, however, that the most salient aspect of Susan's particular journey had been socializing with fellow travelers, a topic we had not explicitly considered. As a result, the interviewer asked questions aimed at exploring the social aspect in-depth. The questions in the guide were also asked because they offered a good temporal framework to navigate the interview but not exactly in the planned order.

Before embarking on a series of interviews, it is advisable to pilot the interview process with a real participant to test the questions and the general flow of the interview and to refine the guide.

How you start the interview is important to make your participant feel at ease and build the trust required for them to talk freely. You can start by explaining that you would like to hear about their experiences, that you consider them the experts, and that there are no right or wrong answers. You will be listening a lot because you hope that they will do most of the talking, and they should take their time to think of their answers and not feel rushed.

During the interview, make sure you allow participants to give full answers, resisting the temptation to ask a new question before you are sure that they have said everything they had to say on the previous one. At times, someone will finish talking and, as they pause, something else will come to mind. You should hold that empty space, not fill it immediately, and to do so, you need to feel comfortable with silence, which is one of the most difficult skills for novice interviewers. If your participant is having difficulties answering, you can, however, step in, perhaps using a prompt or asking for an example. It is important for IPA interviews to be centered on the experience of participants and how they make sense of it. If participants stray toward being more abstract (i.e., talking about experience in general), we recommend using questions to gently bring them back, encouraging them to talk about their specific and concrete experiences.

In comparison to other types of interviews, IPA interviews are in-depth: You are immersing yourself in another person's world and aiming to see their experience through their eyes to make sense of how they understand the world and themselves within it. Reaching the right level of depth requires you to be an attentive listener and probe whenever more could be said about a topic (e.g., "Could you expand on this?"). Often, participants are unsure of the appropriate level at which to position their narrative, so your probing will encourage them to go deeper, and you might find that they will then be able to go there of their own accord.

When you are an insider to the interview topic, meaning that you are familiar with the experience that participants are describing, there might be shared understandings that are taken for granted and remain tacit. For the benefit of your readers, you should ensure that such understandings are made explicit by asking participants to talk as if you knew nothing about the topic.

During the interview, it is crucial to check that the participant is comfortable by watching their nonverbal cues and their responses, particularly if the conversation touches on sensitive topics. Although you are aiming for depth, this must not be achieved at the cost of the participant's well-being, and your ethical duties should always take priority. You should be equally aware and protective of your own well-being; interviews, especially on sensitive topics, can take a toll on the interviewer as well. Keeping a journal is a good way to reflect on your interviewing experience and, if in need, you should consider reaching out for support from your advisor or supervisor or, if it is a more serious concern, a mental health professional.

To give you a sense of how in a live interview you might use the guide and its prompts, while also dynamically probing for depth, let us look at the extract from Susan's transcript in Exhibit 3.2. This passage comes toward the end of the interview where, after a series of questions about her experience abroad, the time has come to discuss Susan's return home (roughly corresponding to Question 10 in Exhibit 3.1).

The first question ("And can you remember when you were still there the thought of the end of this period coming? How did you feel about it?") is a rewording of the first part of Question 10 from the guide (Exhibit 3.1) about how she felt at the prospect of returning home. Because this question opens up a new avenue, Susan, who was not a shy participant, provided a rather long answer. After having given many motivations for returning and explaining why staying was not an option, Susan concluded by stating that she was not really ready to come home. She stopped talking, but the interviewer felt more could be said, so said, "You weren't?" This is not really a question; it is more a way of encouraging Susan to keep talking. At this point, Susan drew a parallel with other times when she had felt ready to return home after being away. The question that follows ("What was it about being there that you didn't want to leave?") is a probe: To achieve more depth and understanding of the motives for Susan's reluctance to return, the interviewer asked an unplanned open question specifically in response to something that Susan had said. As you can see from this short example, the guide is indeed the backbone of the interview, but an interview dynamic is often more fluid and complex than a set of questions and answers.

EXHIBIT 3.2. Extract From Pages 13 and 14 of Susan's Transcript Illustrating an Interview Dynamic

I: *And can you remember when you were still there, the thought of the end of this period coming? How did you feel about it?*

S: Really sad. Because, again, my closest friend I met out there, her name's Sammy and she lives in Reading and my boyfriend used to live in Reading so I used to see her a lot and she, I met her on the first week, the last week we were there, with her friends and I remember it being like, "Ah, are you coming with us to Angkor Wat tomorrow?" and I was like, "I am going home tomorrow," and they were like, "What?" And I was like, "Yeah!" So, my life out there was still, the only reason I came home was because my ex-boyfriend's birthday was the next day and it was like a big birthday, I think, and I wanted to go away again at the end of the year, so I knew I couldn't spend a lot of money there, I had to save it. So that's the reason I came home, it wasn't, it wasn't his fault, it was my decision, but if it wasn't for him I wouldn't have come. I remember, but yeah, it was, it was hard because I felt I wasn't finished, and I was just getting started and they offered me a job at the hostel, and, ahm, so I had like no money at that point and they, "Oh we'll pay for your keep and your food if you stay, and if you're like," I'm quite lively so be a rep or whatever, so I felt like I still had so much that I could do there, but I had to, I had to come home, because I had a flight and I couldn't afford another flight and my parents weren't going to bail me out, if I wanted to stay and have fun, and they're public servants, they're not, you know, they haven't got half a grand for a flight home to give me. So yeah, it was quite hard and going from that to then being in the UK and I wasn't really ready to come home.

I: *You weren't?*

S: No, I wasn't ready to come home, there wasn't, ahm, I went to a few festivals before and the last day I'm always like, "I want to go home now." Like it's a means to an end. [chuckles] I am sick of being here, and I wasn't sick of it. I kind of wanted, so part of, a part of me always wanted to be there.

I: *What was it about being there that you didn't want to leave?*

S: I hadn't finished, ahm, I think, yeah, I hadn't finished meeting the people that I wanted, like, new people, I hadn't finished just doing whatever you wanted to do, I wasn't ready to start work again, I didn't want to go back to my old job, I did in the end, I found it so boring.

Note. I = interviewer; S = Susan.

Interviewing is a skill that takes time to master. We have offered some pointers, but only practice and self-reflection will allow you to hone your technique. If you relisten to and transcribe your pilot interview as soon as possible and review it critically, you can identify areas to be improved for your next interviews. Indeed, it may well be that you do this formally with your supervisor or advisor. Our practice as supervisors is to look closely at the transcript of a student's pilot interview and decide whether it shows sufficient indicators of good practice. If it does, the student can move on to the subsequent interviews, and all can be included in the corpus for analysis. Otherwise, we discuss with the student the good and not-so-good qualities and what to learn for the next interview, which then becomes the first interview proper. Some students get the process straight away. For others, there is a steep learning curve, most commonly between the pilot and other interviews. And, of course, it should be remembered that there is no such thing as a perfect interview: Each interview is a unique encounter between people, with its own alchemy. Therefore, even seasoned IPA interviewers can learn from the interviews they are conducting.

TRANSCRIPTION

You need to produce a verbatim transcript of each interview. Unlike other qualitative methods that require a more detailed and highly codified form of transcription (e.g., conversation analysis; Hepburn & Potter, 2021), IPA is mainly interested in the contents of an interview, so a transcript, including everything that was said by the participant and by the researcher, is considered sufficient. The central column in Exhibit 3.3 contains one page of Susan's transcript. The right and left margins are left blank for the researcher's annotations, as we discuss in more detail in Chapter 4. As you can see in the transcript, at Lines 18 to 22, Susan said something the interviewer did not catch, and she was asked to repeat it. For the most part, such instances are not relevant to the final analysis, but they should be included nonetheless because they could potentially be interesting and give a sense of the flow of the interview (Susan was actually a fast speaker, so the interviewer often asked her to repeat what she said).

The transcript will include all semantic information (literal words spoken by both parties) but not necessarily all prosodic components of speech (related to the rhythmic aspects of language, such as the length of pauses, and so on). It can, however, be useful to include some comments on the major nonverbal aspects of the interview, such as laughter, marked pauses, or changes in tone of voice. In Exhibit 3.3, at Line 33, some prosodic information has been added between square brackets; it will be useful when we subsequently interpret the surrounding text. Similarly, the word "so" in Line 3 has been formatted in bold to indicate a change in tone of voice; when reading it, you can almost hear Susan emphasize just how long the journey had felt to her.

Special software systems and services can help with transcription, particularly when there is a large volume of data to process. Although such tools can be useful, we advocate the value of doing your own transcriptions if you are a novice researcher, particularly for the first few interviews. Transcribing

EXHIBIT 3.3. One Page of Susan's Transcript With Empty Margins to Be Used Later for Analysis

#	Original transcript
1	**I:** And when you first got there, what was the first impression?
2	**S:** It was so different, it was so different and, yeah, it was just
3	busy and also it was really hot, and I'd been traveling **so** long,
4	it must have been, it was 24 hours. I remember going out for
5	dinner the first night on my own, because obviously I was
6	staying alone, I was staying in a hotel that I had booked,
7	because I didn't want to stay in a hostel that night, because
8	obviously I want to just have a shower, sort myself out and get
9	used to jet lag and stuff, I went for dinner that night on my
10	own, it was fine, and I met these Danish girls, I remember
11	being really nervous, because that's the first thing I remember
12	thinking was, "I've got to put myself out there, I can't just sit
13	and," that night I was like, "'Hi" and they were chatting to me
14	but I was a bit reserved, I remember thinking, ahm, that's the
15	first thing I thought, like I've got to, if I'm going to do this,
16	and do what I want to, I can't just sit back, I need to really
17	make an effort, so that was kind of quite a big thought, in my
18	mind the first night I was there. To get out of my comfort zone
19	a bit.
20	**I:** Say that again.
21	**S:** Get out of my comfort zone, yeah.

22	**I:**	And?
23	**S:**	It worked, I guess! Ahm, ahm, that's one thing I didn't
24		really think about because not a lot of people, ahm, when I was
25		telling this to my family, well I'm from a little village in
26		Northshire, so, you know, my mom and dad are quite liberal,
27		but my grandparents and my family were like, "Oh, you're
28		going on your own," and I was only 18 and, just turned really,
29		I told them and they were like, "Oh, you're going on your
30		own," and I was like, "yeah!" I didn't think it was that big a
31		thing and I went out there and not a lot of people were solo.
32		That's what they call it, like, solo travelers or whatever
33		[chuckles]. Not a lot of people were, and I didn't, again, I
34		wasn't expecting **that**, I was expecting people to be on their
35		own and even when I saw people there, they were like, "Oh,
36		you're on your own?" And I was like "yeah, like, just doing
37		my thing." And they were just like "oh!" So, I was kind of
38		expecting more people to be on their own, so, when you're in a
39		group you're less likely to speak to other people, so I really
40		had to put in the effort and judge people quite quickly as well.
41		So, yeah, I just had to put stuff out there quite a lot, but that
42		wasn't what I was expecting, I thought people would just be
43		like, "I'm solo too, let's hang out." But it was a bit, it wasn't
44		hard, but it definitely was different to what I thought.

Note. I = interviewer; S = Susan.

is an important stage because it allows you to become deeply familiar with the data and review your interview technique. If you choose not to transcribe the interviews yourself, make sure you always check the transcription carefully against the audio file.

Transcribing is also a good time to anonymize the data. To make a transcript truly anonymous, it is not enough to replace the participant's name with a pseudonym; you should also change the names of any person they mention and any other potentially identifying information, such as the name of their employer or specific locations and events.

Having collected and transcribed your data, you are now ready to analyze it, a process during which you, as a researcher, are given the opportunity to deeply engage with your data to uncover and illuminate the phenomenon under investigation and its meanings to participants.

4

ANALYZING THE DATA

Starting With the First Case

There are some fundamental principles in the interpretative phenomeno-logical analysis (IPA) analytical process. Interpretation is central, with a particular focus on understanding the participant's point of view and how they make sense of their experiences. Also important is maintaining an idiographic and inductive approach so that the data for each participant are analyzed on their own terms and as free as possible from theoretical constraints. Finally, the process is iterative so that each stage can potentially lead to revising prior interpretative decisions.

Such a flexible view of the analysis is suitable for an experienced researcher but can be rather daunting for those who are starting out. In this book, we, therefore, break down the analytical process into building blocks and present them in a linear fashion in the belief that giving a structure to follow is the best way to guide neophytes through the complexities of doing analysis with IPA. As you become more experienced and confident, you might develop a more fluid and personalized style of engaging with your data.

IPA's idiographic approach requires data for each person to be fully ana-lyzed on their own terms by performing a single case analysis of each tran-script. This entails engaging in depth with the transcript, making exploratory

https://doi.org/10.1037/0000259-004
Essentials of Interpretative Phenomenological Analysis, by J. A. Smith and I. E. Nizza

notes on the participant's account, identifying experiential statements from the notes, clustering or grouping those into a logical structure, and constructing an individual table of personal experiential themes for the case.[1]

Before exploring the analysis process in detail, it is worth remembering the implications of IPA's interpretative nature and double hermeneutic. You will be reporting your understanding of the participant's description of and reasoning about their experience rather than capturing a pure experience in itself. Because your role as analyst is acknowledged, this should encourage you as a researcher to move beyond a merely descriptive reading of your data toward a more interpretative one, but it should also remind you that because your analysis is interpretative, any claims you make should be presented cautiously. However, IPA offers a rigorous set of procedures that enables the claims you make to be evidence based, thus increasing the validity of your work. See Chapter 8 for more information on methodological integrity in IPA.

There is not a single necessarily correct IPA. The aim of the analysis process and the write-up that is presented is to proceed through a systematic series of steps that are recorded in such a way that someone else could review the audit trail of that process. The aim of that audit is to check that the analysis presented is warranted as a result of the documented analysis process. The audit may be conducted by an independent researcher. For novice researchers, the advisor or supervisor, in effect, takes on some of this role. Thinking of preparing for an independent audit is a powerful idea. Even if an audit does not actually take place, it is good practice for researchers to keep all of their work in an order that would allow somebody to check the complete research process.

STEP 1: READING AND EXPLORATORY NOTES

Before engaging in a detailed analysis of any transcript, it is good practice to read through the transcript at least once while relistening to the recording. Especially if some time has passed since the data were gathered, listening

---

[1]As we explained in Chapter 1, we have modified some of the terminology involved in describing the process of analysis in IPA. The main change is that what used to be called *emergent themes* are now described as *experiential statements*. We believe this is a better term for this stage of the process. The other change we are making is a clearer delineation of our use of the term *theme* in subsequent stages. In simple terms, a collection of experiential statements is clustered to form a personal experiential theme. How this works is explained in detail in this chapter. We advise newcomers to IPA to use the new terminology. If you are already well into a study, you can discuss with your advisor or supervisor whether to change your terminology or stick with the older terms. We recognize that, for a time, both sets of terms will be in circulation.

will place you back into the interview context and rekindle your memory so that, later in the analysis, the participant's voice will be evoked by reading their words. Initial reading may also give you a sense of the structure of the narrative and how the various components fit with each other.

While reading through the transcript, one records one's initial reactions to the text in one margin. This is a pretty nonprescriptive process—you comment on anything you think is of interest or importance as you are reading. It is also not so important how you express your responses at this first stage—first impressions can be refined later. There are no rules on how many notes you should make; some areas warrant more comments than others, depending on the density and richness of the text or your interpretation of it. You should aim to read the text slowly, thoroughly, and in depth rather than superficially. While commenting, try to keep an open mind, looking beyond what you expected to find, staying with the participant's words, reflecting on them, and trying not to jump to conclusions. You will be looking for similarities and differences between portions of text and magnifications or contradictions in the participant's words, focusing on single words or sentences, questioning your response to them, and attempting to understand what they meant to the participant. Exhibit 4.1 shows a commented portion of the transcript with the notes presented alongside and in line with the text being referred to. Normally, such notes will be the fruit of multiple readings, with new notes added as new insights develop.

We advise students to make their notes by hand on a hard copy of the transcript, formatted with wide margins, as shown in Exhibit 4.1. The notes should go in one margin (usually the right one), keeping the other margin clear for formulating experiential statements during the next stage. Some researchers prefer to comment directly on an electronic version of the transcript, using a word processor; it is a question of personal preference. Whether you comment on paper or electronically, it can be useful to underline key passages or circle key words. While data analysis computer software packages are available to support qualitative analysis, we see them as more valuable for methods employing a larger data corpus. We are not saying they cannot be used with IPA; however, we would not recommend using such tools in IPA when you are still learning the ropes.

Although there is no one correct set of exploratory notes for any transcript, some find it useful to differentiate between three types of notes: descriptive, linguistic, and conceptual (Smith et al., 2009). These approaches should be considered as a way of helping you think more in depth about what the transcript contains. They can be combined

EXHIBIT 4.1. Recording Exploratory Notes

#		Original transcript	Exploratory notes
1	**I:**	And when you first got there, what was the first impression?	Remembering her initial sensations
2	**S:**	It was so different, it was so different and, yeah, it was just	repetition of 'different': *can't find suitable words?*
3		busy and also it was really hot, and I'd been traveling **so** long,	busy, really hot: struck by physical difference
4		it must have been, it was 24 hours. I remember going out for	traveling **so** long: *is she emphasizing how alien it all*
5		dinner the first night on my own, because obviously I was	*felt?*
6		staying alone, I was staying in a hotel that I had booked,	Chose to spend the first night in a hotel to adjust to
7		because I didn't want to just have a shower, sort myself out and get	the destination
8		obviously I want to just have a shower, sort myself out and get	
9		used to jet lag and stuff, I went for dinner that night on my	On my own, it was fine: *her need to say this suggests*
10		own, it was fine, and I met these Danish girls, I remember	*perhaps it wasn't so fine?*
11		being really nervous, because that's the first thing I remember	She immediately started to link up with other people:
12		thinking was, "I've got to put myself out there, I can't just sit	first encounter with some Danish girls
13		and," that night I was like, "Hi" and they were chatting to me	She made the first move but found it difficult to engage
14		but I was a bit reserved, I remember thinking, ahm, that's the	fully (reserved): *why?*
15		first thing I thought, like I've got to, if I'm going to do this,	I've got to: *considers socializing a necessary step to*
16		and do what I want to, I can't just sit back, I need to really	*achieve the holiday she wants, however hard it feels*
17		make an effort, so that was kind of quite a big thought, in my	big thought: top priority
18		mind the first night I was there. To get out of my comfort zone	*Socializing wasn't natural to her, it was effortful, she*
19		a bit.	*had to push herself.*
20	**I:**	Say that again.	
21	**S:**	Get out of my comfort zone, yeah.	

22	I:	And?
23	**S:**	It worked, I guess! Ahm, ahm, that's one thing I didn't
24		really think about because not a lot of people, ahm, when I was	Many false starts: she's finding it difficult to express *this concept – is it because today she realizes the abnormality of her situation?*
25		telling this to my family, well I'm from a little village in	
26		Northshire, so, you know, my mom and dad are quite liberal,	I was only 18: emphasizing her young age
27		but my grandparents and my family were like, "Oh, you're	Her family expressed perplexities but she did not
28		going on your own," and I was only 18 and, just turned really,	understand at the time, then realized how unusual it was.
29		I told them and they were like, "Oh, you're going on your	yeah!: very flippant response *We get a sense here of*
30		own," and I was like, "yeah!" I didn't think it was that big a	*how independent from her family she feels*
31		thing and I went out there and not a lot of people were solo.	
32		That's what they call it, like, solo travelers or whatever	
33		[chuckles]. Not a lot of people were, and I didn't, again, I	
34		wasn't expecting **that**, I was expecting people to be on their	emphasized 'that': Surprised at discovering her
35		own and even when I saw people there, they were like, "Oh,	expectations did not match reality.
36		you're on your own?" And I was like "yeah, like, just doing	On your own: even other travelers were surprised by
37		my thing." And they were just like "oh!" So, I was kind of	her solo travel
38		expecting more people to be on their own, so, when you're in a	*Doing my thing: another flippant response, she seems*
39		group you're less likely to speak to other people, so I really	*defensive, is she covering the realization that she needs*
40		had to put in the effort and judge people quite quickly as well.	*a strategy to protect herself?*
41		So, yeah, I just had to put stuff out there quite a lot, but that	had: effortful necessity; quite quickly: pressure to
42		wasn't what I was expecting, I thought people would just be	get it right; put stuff out there: communicating
43		like, "I'm solo too, let's hang out." But it was a bit, it wasn't	more than she normally would
44		hard, but it definitely was different to what I thought.	*Performing to get friends and not travel solo?*

Note. I = interviewer; S = Susan.

and linked with each other so that, for example, a certain way of saying something may lead you to question the motivations behind the choice of words, identify potential meanings, and formulate conceptualizations. Let us review in more detail what these different types of notes can reveal by using examples from the annotated portion of the transcript in Exhibit 4.1.

Descriptive Notes

For any transcript, there will be some basic notes to summarize the explicit meaning of what the participant has said and describe what things matter to them, in terms of objects, events, experiences, processes, locations, principles, and so on. The aim is to identify the elements that structure the participant's thoughts and experiences, taking them at face value.

In Exhibit 4.1, these types of notes appear in the right column as plain text (as opposed to the underlined and italicized notes that we describe later). For example, the notes on Line 1, "Remembering her initial sensations," and Lines 6 and 7, "Chose to spend the first night in a hotel to adjust to the destination," are a summary of what is described in the corresponding paragraphs. Similarly, the "even other travelers were surprised by her solo travel" note at Lines 36 and 37 is descriptive because it refers to the questions that Susan reported receiving from fellow travelers but is formulated at a higher level of abstraction because it contains an inference (i.e., she never explicitly says they were surprised). Some descriptive notes may appear redundant or not contributing particularly to the analysis, yet the act of writing them is a way of ensuring you understand at a basic level what is happening in that portion of the transcript.

Linguistic Notes

The use of language, meaning the actual words spoken or how they are spoken, can also be commented on. Certain linguistic aspects are considered particularly interesting, such as the use of pronouns, verb tenses, pauses, laughter, repetitions, hesitations, and tone, so they are often used to inform the interpretation. For instance, a change from using the first person to using the second or third person in the narrative can be an indicator of a topic being particularly critical for the speaker (often, this switch is interpreted as a distancing strategy). False starts can indicate something that the participant is finding difficult to put into words and, therefore, may be of particular importance to them. A false start occurs when the participant starts to say something but starts a new phrase before completing the first one. For example, at Line 24 in Exhibit 4.1 (where linguistic notes appear underlined), we have annotated with the note "<u>Many false starts</u>." Susan seems to hesitate when explaining that her decision to travel solo while being only 18 had raised perplexities in her family that she had originally dismissed. This could be an indication of her difficulty in admitting that her family was right, given that she later felt vulnerable and felt the need to find other groups of people with whom to travel.

Metaphors are figures of speech to notice while commenting because they are recognized as having the ability to help participants communicate and share experiences that are otherwise difficult to convey (Shinebourne & Smith, 2010). For instance, at one point elsewhere in her interview, Susan used the term "quick-clip" to describe an encounter she had with some girls who eventually became close friends. Quick-clip is a type of fastening that is particularly fast and easy to activate, so the term symbolizes her immediate attraction and fast and firm bonding with the girls. The immediacy of their bond was a relief for Susan but was also problematic because she felt torn between feeling comfortable with them and keeping to her own travel aims. Using the quick-clip metaphor, she effectively captured how easy it was to bond with the girls and what an effort it was for her to break away from them.

Here we are paying close attention to the actual words of the participant and how they were expressed. How is this different from a linguistic discursive analysis? The difference lies in the fact that while we are indeed conducting a detailed linguistic analysis, it is to inform our understanding of the cognitive and affective state of the person. We are looking closely at their words to help our analysis of how they are making meaning from their experience. By contrast, a discourse analysis would be concerned with how the speaker constructs their response. This might be interpreted in terms of the conversational intent of the person as they try to make a persuasive case, or it might be considered a manifestation of the linguistic resources available to this person in this particular cultural milieu.

Conceptual Notes

This type of commenting often takes the form of questions, particularly at the start of the analytical process when an overall sense of the data has yet to develop. Some questions may not get further developed, and others may eventually find an answer as the analysis goes deeper and the interpretation takes form. Conceptual comments appear in italics in the example in Exhibit 4.1. For example, for the question at Lines 13–14 (Why did she find it difficult to engage?), no answer is forthcoming at this stage in the analysis, while the question at Line 44 about performing turns out to be important and contributes toward Susan's bonding with strangers eventually becoming an experiential statement, as we shall see in the next step of the analysis.

Conceptual comments typically shift away from the explicit claims of participants and instead consider their and your understanding of what is being discussed overall. The purpose is not to judge what is being said but to be open and consider the participant's standpoint. These notes usually take time to be produced; they require reflection and the formulation of tentative ideas that are refined gradually. Of course, interpretations will be influenced by your professional knowledge and/or personal experience. However, more important, they must be initiated or prompted by your curious reading of what the participant is actually saying. And you should keep in mind that the purpose is not necessarily to find answers or obtain the ultimate understanding but rather to consider a range of potential meanings. For example, the initial notes for Lines 34 to 44 in Exhibit 4.1 focused on Susan's discovery that traveling solo was uncommon. It was only during a subsequent and more considered review that some previously neglected terms such as "had to" and "judge people quite quickly" came into focus, giving rise to the idea that Susan's socializing might have been a self-protective strategy ("had" conveying a sense of obligation, and having to judge people quickly suggesting both the urgency of finding companions and the awareness that not all people would be suitable).

This description of note taking is not intended to be prescriptive or exhaustive; the actual notes are less important than the deep engagement with the data they require, the exploration of potential meanings, and the conceiving of deep interpretations that producing them can generate. And to reiterate, there is no requirement to separate one's responses into the three types of notes outlined earlier. You may prefer to make your comments without differentiating what type of note they are. The style a researcher adopts for exploratory notes is highly personal and reflects their way of thinking and may also change in the course of the analysis.

STEP 2: FORMULATING EXPERIENTIAL STATEMENTS

At the end of the noting phase, you will have a series of exploratory notes down one margin that speak to the transcript and that form the basis from which you will then formulate experiential statements. While during noting you were free to comment in any way you wished, writing experiential statements requires a different mode. The task now is to capture in a succinct form what we have learned about the meaning of the experience to the participant in this portion of text. For each of the participant's speaking turns in the interview, you should aim to identify one or more experiential statements. Each statement could correspond to more than one line, some lines may not map onto a statement, and others may map onto more than one statement. This phase requires an analytic effort because you will need to decide which aspects should be brought to the fore.

Each experiential statement should be a concise summary of what emerges as important in the notes associated with the corresponding portion of the transcript. Statements need to be sufficiently specific to be grounded in the data but also conceptual so that they capture the psychological substance of a text. Statements need to be dense and rich—pointing to both the important psychological process and the context or content of that process being invoked by the participant's response. We have found that some novice researchers sometimes produce statements that, rather than being open phrases, are blunt and closed categories (e.g., "The environment"), which is insufficient to point to what is happening. Instead, the experiential statement should be a phrase or a sentence (e.g., "being struck by the environment") that tells us more about the psychological dynamic that is implicated. Thus, you can see that verbs, adjectives, and nouns all make a useful contribution in the construction of experiential statements.

Let us review the experiential statements defined for the portion of the transcript we have seen and that are added in the left column in Exhibit 4.2. The first one, "Initially struck by environmental difference," is mainly descriptive and was created to represent Susan's physical memories of her holiday experience. The next statement, "Pushing herself out of her comfort zone by being social," captures Susan's psychological experience of forcing herself to socialize.

The next two statements, "Ignored family's perplexity at her traveling solo plans" and "Expected solo travel to be more common," capture the fact that despite her family's questioning of her travel choices, Susan decided to do what she wanted and was surprised at discovering that solo travel was unusual. There is an argument for combining these because they are different aspects of the same process (rejecting her family's objections to discover that they were right); however, there is also value in leaving them separate for the moment until it becomes clearer what direction the overall analysis is going to take. For instance, the relationship with her parents could become a key aspect of the analysis, or the traveling solo could become an important

EXHIBIT 4.2. Adding Experiential Statements in the Left Column

Experiential statement	#	Original transcript	Exploratory notes
	1	**I:** And when you first got there, what was the first impression?	Remembering her initial sensations
Initially struck by environmental difference	2	**S:** It was so different, it was so different and, yeah, it was just	repetition of 'different': *can't find suitable words?*
	3	busy and also it was really hot, and I'd been traveling **so** long,	busy, really hot: struck by physical difference
	4	it must have been, it was 24 hours. I remember going out for	traveling **so** long: *is she emphasizing how alien it all felt?*
	5	dinner the first night on my own, because obviously I was	
	6	staying alone, I was staying in a hotel that I had booked,	Chose to spend the first night in a hotel to adjust to the destination
	7	because I didn't want to stay in a hostel that night, because	
	8	obviously I want to just have a shower, sort myself out and get	
	9	used to jet lag and stuff, I went for dinner that night on my	On my own, it was fine: *her need to say this suggests perhaps it wasn't so fine?*
	10	own, it was fine, and I met these Danish girls, I remember	She immediately started to link up with other people: first encounter with some Danish girls
	11	being really nervous, because that's the first thing I remember	
	12	thinking was, "I've got to put myself out there, I can't just sit	She made the first move but found it difficult to engage fully (reserved): *why?*
Pushing herself out of her comfort zone by being social	13	and," that night I was like, "Hi" and they were chatting to me	
	14	but I was a bit reserved, I remember thinking, ahm, that's the	
	15	first thing I thought, like I've got to, if I'm going to do this,	I've got to: *considers socializing a necessary step to achieve the holiday she wants, however hard it feels*
	16	and do what I want to, I can't just sit back, I need to really	
	17	make an effort, so that was kind of quite a big thought, in my	big thought: top priority
	18	mind the first night I was there. To get out of my comfort zone	Socializing wasn't natural to her, it was effortful, she had to push herself.
	19	a bit.	
	20	**I:** Say that again.	
	21	**S:** Get out of my comfort zone, yeah.	

Ignored family's perplexity at her traveling solo plans	22	**I:** And?	
	23	**S:** It worked, I guess! Ahm, ahm, that's one thing I didn't	Many false starts: she's finding it difficult to express
	24	really think about because not a lot of people, ahm, when I was	this concept – *is it because today she realizes the*
	25	telling this to my family, well I'm from a little village in	*abnormality of her situation?*
	26	Northshire, so, you know, my mom and dad are quite liberal,	
	27	but my grandparents and my family were like, "Oh, you're	I was only 18: emphasizing her young age
	28	going on your own," and I was only 18 and, just turned really,	Her family expressed perplexities but she did not
	29	I told them and they were like, "Oh, you're going on your	understand at the time, then realized how unusual it was.
	30	own," and I was like, "yeah!" I didn't think it was that big a	Yeah!: very flippant response *We get a sense here of*
Expected solo travel to be more common	31	thing and I went out there and not a lot of people were solo.	*how independent from her family she feels*
	32	That's what they call it, like, solo travelers or whatever	
	33	[chuckles]. Not a lot of people were, and I didn't, again, I	
	34	wasn't expecting **that**, I was expecting people to be on their	emphasized 'that': Surprised at discovering her
	35	own and even when I saw people there, they were like, "Oh,	expectations did not match reality.
	36	you're on your own?" And I was like "yeah, like, just doing	On your own: even other travelers were surprised by
Selectively and purposively bonding with strangers	37	my thing." And they were just like "oh!" So, I was kind of	her solo travel
	38	expecting more people to be on their own, so, when you're in	Doing my thing: another flippant response, *she seems*
	39	a group you're less likely to speak to other people, so I really	*defensive, is she covering the realization that she needs a*
	40	had to put in the effort and judge people quite quickly as well.	*strategy to protect herself?*
	41	So, yeah, I just had to put stuff out there quite a lot, but that	Had to: effortful necessity; quite quickly: pressure to
	42	wasn't what I was expecting, I thought people would just be	get it right; put stuff out there: communicating
	43	like, "I'm solo too, let's hang out." But it was a bit, it wasn't	more than she normally would
	44	hard, but it definitely was different to what I thought.	*Performing to get friends and not travel solo?*

Note. I = interviewer; S = Susan.

aspect, independent of her parents' opinion. This is an example of how the analyst works in an iterative way, pondering interpretative decisions and evaluating at what level of detail to position each experiential statement, considering both a local and a wider perspective on the text.

The final statement in Exhibit 4.2, "Selectively and purposively bonding with strangers," is the most interpretative of all in this example. It is grounded in the text (Susan does describe selecting people and bonding with them); however, it is also highly interpretative because it is based on an overall understanding of Susan's travel strategies as serving a purpose, going a little beyond what Susan actually said. Never in her interview did she say that her decision to travel with others was due to the challenges of traveling on her own, yet the interview was permeated with signs that lead in this direction. The task for the analyst is to pick up on these signs and use them to reveal the underlying psychological mechanism by defining experiential statements that build on such signs. In this case, Susan used the verb "had to" (Lines 40 and 41) and, earlier in the transcript, said "I've got to put myself out there" (Line 12), both instances suggesting a lack of choice, an inevitability in her decision to bond with strangers that (we assume) was the result of her challenges traveling solo. This is quite a bold interpretation but also a plausible one that the analyst will need to reevaluate and possibly build a case for as the analysis progresses to the next stages.

Most experiential statements will be tightly connected to a particular place in the transcript. Sometimes such statements can themselves include a referent to how this statement is elaborating or contradicting something that has come before.

Overall, developing experiential statements requires a condensing effort to allow both the important aspects of the participant's experience and the analyst's understanding of that experience to emerge. As previously, it takes time, deep engagement with the data, and reflection to define well-worded and meaningful statements that go beyond a purely descriptive account, privileging a more interpretative one. Although it can be daunting, there is reassurance in the fact that any decision you take can, and probably will, be reviewed later because the IPA process is iterative.

STEP 3: FINDING CONNECTIONS AND CLUSTERING EXPERIENTIAL STATEMENTS

Once you have identified experiential statements for the whole interview, you will have a long list of statements to work with, each associated with a specific portion of the transcript. To give you an idea of the volume to expect, the analysis of Susan's entire transcript produced over a hundred statements. Your actual number will depend on the length of the interview, types of topics discussed, and density of the statements you identified. In this third stage of the analysis, the aim is to review and refine the experiential statements, putting like with like, distilling, synthesizing, and identifying a structure that can bring them together. You are constantly aiming to build and refine the analysis to show more clearly the key features of the experience the participant has undergone and the key sense making that they have engaged in.

Our preferred approach to clustering is to create a list of the experiential statements, print it out, cut the sheet up so that each statement is on a separate piece of paper, and then place all the pieces randomly on a large surface where they can be easily repositioned (e.g., a board, a large table, the floor). By working this way, you will have a bird's-eye view of all the experiential statements and be able to shift them around, grouping them in different ways while obtaining a spatial representation of the grouping.

The main question one is asking when clustering is "What should go with what?" As you may imagine, the answer depends on what experiential statements are available but also on what the research question is and your thinking about the data because clustering is itself an interpretative activity.

So far, we have five experiential statements—the ones generated for the passage in Exhibit 4.2:

- Initially struck by environmental difference,
- Pushing herself out of her comfort zone by being social,
- Ignored family's perplexity at her traveling solo plans,
- Expected solo travel to be more common, and
- Selectively and purposively bonding with strangers.

To help illustrate the process of clustering, we have compiled these with some of the other experiential statements generated from Susan's interview transcript in Exhibit 4.3. The statements are listed in the order in which they appeared on the transcript.

So now imagine each of these written on a separate piece of paper spread out randomly on the work surface in front of you. You start to shift them around, bringing together the statements that you think are similar or connected in some way. So, for instance, you might see how "Pushing herself out of her comfort zone by being social" and "Selectively and purposively bonding with strangers" both concern how Susan tried to get close to the new people she met while traveling, so it makes sense to bring them together. Accordingly, you position the corresponding pieces of paper close to each other. You then continue to cluster by gradually reviewing the experiential

EXHIBIT 4.3. Subset of Experiential Statements From Susan's Transcript

Travel motivated by a desire to escape own constrained reality

Much focus on leaving, less on destination

Initially struck by environmental difference

Pushing herself out of her comfort zone by being social

Ignored family's perplexity at her traveling solo plans

Expected solo travel to be more common

Selectively and purposively bonding with strangers

Forced to trust strangers while having no control over her situation

Following the flow of others as a necessity and as a limitation

When backpacking you have closer boundaries with strangers

Flashes of awareness of own vulnerability

Fear inspired by media discourses on female solo traveler risks

Fear of being abducted

Wanting to avoid potentially risky situations

Realizing she had been incautious

statements one by one, shifting them around and bringing them together into groupings that make sense to you. We did this with the statements listed in Exhibit 4.3, and you can see how we have clustered them in Exhibit 4.4.

As you can see in Exhibit 4.4, we created three clusters labeled A, B, and C. The first cluster, A, relates to Susan's expectations before she set out and how she perceived her travel as a point of departure, an opportunity to break away from the reality of her "normal life." We obtained this cluster by bringing together the two experiential statements related to solo travel that emerged from the portion of the transcript we showed you earlier ("Expected solo travel to be more common" and "Ignored family's perplexity at her traveling solo plans") with other statements from elsewhere in the transcript that talked about Susan's motivations to travel.

Cluster B includes experiential statements that emerged from areas of the transcript that we have not shown you. They all related to Susan's developing awareness, as she was traveling, of her vulnerability as a young female solo traveler.

Last, Cluster C includes two more of the experiential statements that you are already familiar with, illustrating how Susan actively sought the company of strangers and bonded with them, with others that discuss the consequences of the bonding and Susan's ideas about what happens when you travel with somebody else. Some of these statements are clearly similar to each other, while others almost seem to be working in contrast. Bringing them together

EXHIBIT 4.4. Clustering of Experiential Statements

A

Travel motivated by a desire to escape own constrained reality

Much focus on leaving, less on destination

Expected solo travel to be more common

Ignored family's perplexity at her traveling solo plans

B

Flashes of awareness of own vulnerability

Realizing she had been incautious

Wanting to avoid potentially risky situations

Fear of being abducted

Fear inspired by media discourses on female solo traveler risks

C

Pushing herself out of her comfort zone by being social

Selectively and purposively bonding with strangers

When backpacking you have closer boundaries with strangers

Forced to trust strangers while having no control over her situation

Following the flow of others as a necessity and as a limitation

shows how Susan had complex and mixed feelings about traveling with others: She sought them out but also recognized the limitations that her choice not to be alone entailed. From an interpretative point of view, this cluster is one of the most interesting aspects of her analysis: The idea that her behavior was driven by needs that she did not totally acknowledge and that, to a certain extent, she resented having. From a methodological perspective, the cluster illustrates how, when clustering and bringing together experiential statements, we might be looking for similarities between statements and also differences.

STEP 4: COMPILING THE TABLE OF PERSONAL EXPERIENTIAL THEMES

Once the clustering feels satisfactory and meaningful, it can be converted into a table of personal experiential themes where each cluster is named as a personal experiential theme, and identifying information for all the experiential statements contained within each theme is given. See Exhibit 4.5, where we have done this for our clusters from Exhibit 4.4.

EXHIBIT 4.5. Table of Personal Experiential Themes From Susan's Analysis

	Page/line	Quotes
Theme 1. Expectations of travel as a mark of independence		
Travel motivated by a desire to escape own constrained reality	1.20	*I wanted to go away.*
Much focus on leaving, less on destination	3.7	*I didn't really think about it.*
Expected solo travel to be more common	4.33	*Not a lot of people were . . .*
Ignored family's perplexity at her traveling solo plans	4.30	*I was like, "yeah!"*
Theme 2. Becoming aware of own vulnerability		
Flashes of awareness of own vulnerability	24.20	*Like a snap, I should be careful.*
Realizing she had been incautious	26.7	*What could have happened?*
Wanting to avoid potentially risky situations	26.1	*I didn't want to be . . .*
Fear of being abducted	25.5	*I said, "Oh, stop the car."*
Fear inspired by media discourses on female solo traveler risks	25.13	*This is the perfect news story.*
Theme 3. Travel companions: A tension between wanting company and staying in control		
Pushing herself out of her comfort zone by being social	4.16	*I can't just sit back.*
Selectively and purposively bonding with strangers	4.40	*I really had to put in the effort.*
When backpacking you have closer boundaries with strangers	19.9	*You're sharing a room with them.*
Forced to trust strangers while having no control over her situation	8.12	*Had to trust him.*
Following the flow of others as a necessity and as a limitation	11.18	*Gone with their flow.*

The title of each personal experiential theme is an expression of the convergence as the experiential statements are brought together. Hopefully, you can see how the thinking process involved in clustering each set of statements, which we described earlier, in turn, led to the titles we have given to those clusters as personal experiential themes. Note that it is also possible to refer to personal experiential themes as PETs. For each experiential statement contained under a theme, you should indicate the page or line number(s) on which it occurs and present key words from the transcript at this point. This is part of documenting the evidence trail—showing you where you obtained the statement and reminding you what the participant said that prompted it. This will be useful later in the analysis and writing-up process.

SOME MORE THOUGHTS ON CLUSTERING AND COMPILING

As we said earlier, we have presented the process with a manageable subset of experiential statements so you can clearly see the steps we went through. This illustrates the core building blocks in the process. Usually, however, you will have many more statements than illustrated here, so how does the process work in this case?

First, there may be some repetition or redundancy in the clustering process. As you pull experiential statements together, you may notice that you have given exactly, or more or less, the same name for more than one statement. The repeated instances can be taken off the table or board, but you may find it useful to compile a note of them. Alternatively, you can stack multiple instances of an experiential statement on top of each other and move the stack around as you cluster.

Next, another level of compacting may ensue when experiential statements that are close to illustrating the same thing can be merged, either under one existing statement or by a slight rewording of an experiential statement.

The clustering process may well have led you to have a large number of clusters in the first round. For example, you might start with 100 experiential statements and organize them into 10 clusters with 10 statements per cluster. This initial clustering enables you to differentiate the wood from the trees. As a result, you might now be able "to cluster the clusters," putting related groupings together, resulting in, say, five larger clusters.

You can then take each cluster in turn and review the set of statements it contains and see what further organization is possible. There are indeed a number of possibilities. It may be that now that one is operating at a slightly higher conceptual level, another round of redundancies comes into play where it is clear that a number of experiential statements are saying similar things and can therefore be combined. Let us imagine, at this point, we see there are three statements expressed in similar terms. We might decide to retain the best statement to speak for the subgroup and discard the others, or we might decide to reexpress a statement slightly differently to capture the experience of the three statements. Either way, we now have one statement in the cluster that is doing the work of the three with which we started.

Relatedly, it may be that as this level of clustering has enabled you to think of the experience of the participant at quite a high conceptual level, you decide some statements are no longer contributing sufficiently to that analysis and can therefore be taken out. Actually, we have already seen an instance of this. You may have noticed that "Initially struck by environmental difference" that was in Exhibit 4.3 does not appear in the Exhibit 4.4 clustering. This is because it was not related to any other statement, nor did it seem to be doing particularly important analytic work, so it was dropped.

Finally, when documenting your clusters as personal experiential themes, you should attempt to put the statements within the cluster in an order, which could, for example, represent a chronology illustrating the passage of time or a taxonomy illustrating the different features of the cluster. If there are quite a lot of statements in the clustered theme, it may be that this process leads to the emergence of a subclustering organization where the overall personal experiential theme is divided into a small set of subthemes.

Thus, clustering is a careful but creative process, and there is no single right way to do it. Earlier, we described some of the techniques that can help this process. It is good practice to keep a log of your analytical process and any decisions you make during the analysis because you might want to revisit them. Such a log will also become useful when you write up and describe the analytical procedures in the methods section of your project report (see Chapter 6).

It is also possible to try going through the clustering process a number of times. It is now easy to photographically record a clustering by, for example, using a smartphone camera. You can then, maybe with the assistance of your advisor or supervisor, decide which organizational clustering best captures an account of the participant's personal experience.

Whichever techniques you use, you should be working to distill and order your set of experiential statements into a coherent and manageable pattern. We usually think of an optimal table of personal experiential themes as including between three to five themes, with each theme having three to five experiential statements, or if there are a larger number of statements in a particular theme, this will usually be organized into a set of subthemes.

These numbers are indicative and not prescriptive, and the goal should be quality, not quantity. The overall aim of the analysis is to tell the reader, or listener, the detailed story of, let us say, the three to five most important things we have learned about how the participant experienced the phenomenon under investigation. These most important things are the personal experiential themes.

And then, because we are doing an idiographic analysis, we want to be able to talk about the different characteristics recounted by the participant in describing each of those most important experiential features. These different characteristics are represented by the statements in each personal experiential theme.

Look at Exhibit 4.5 again. We said at the time that this is just the result of clustering a subset of experiential statements. Therefore, the outcome of the clustering of all the statements that came up in Susan's analysis will be a larger and different table. However, that final table will have a similar shape to the one in Exhibit 4.5, which serves, therefore, both as the logical outcome of the small-scale analysis we conducted and as an exemplar of what the final table of personal experiential themes for the case will look like.

We like working in the way described here and encourage newcomers to work in a similar way. Placing individual experiential statements on a table or the floor has the effect of giving all of them equivalent status rather than privileging any. Thus, any statement may then be moved to link with any other statement. Any statement can act as a magnet pulling other statements toward it.

An alternative is to work using a spreadsheet or a word processor, color coding experiential statements and shifting them around in the file. While the technology looks helpful here, you need to be careful. There is a danger in working on the computer that one loses the equivalence we have described in the last paragraph. For example, in contrast to what we have pictured, experiential statements early in the list are in danger of being privileged as one scans for other statements similar to the early ones seen. This is not inevitable, but we do caution care if you proceed in this way. Some more specialist packages or mind-mapping software can be used to develop and represent connections between statements creatively.

ONE CASE OR MORE THAN ONE CASE?

It is possible to write up an IPA single case study. This may be done for a number of reasons. When learning IPA, it can be valuable to go through all stages in the research process to familiarize yourself with the complete research cycle. In this case, your supervisor may advise you to write up the first case as an entity in its own right before moving to the analysis of the whole corpus. One may decide to do this also if one has obtained data from a single participant that is either extremely unusual or novel or extremely rich, or the analysis of that case is especially potent. The rationale here is that the write-up of the single case is itself making a significant contribution to the literature. And indeed, this completeness and complexity of that contribution could be compromised by subsuming the analysis of this case into that of the whole corpus.

If your project has just this single case, you will then move from the table of personal experiential themes to writing up the study (see Chapter 6), using the table you have produced as a structure to write up the results. However, if you have a number of participants in your study, you will now put the first completed case aside and move to the second case, continuing with the analysis of each case in turn.

In reality, analyzing a single case is quite unusual. More commonly, we analyze and write up data from a number of participants. The outcome of this process is a document that offers an analysis of the patterning across the group as a whole while at the same time pointing to the nuance and variability in the way that patterning is displayed for particular individuals.

The aim with IPA, in keeping with an idiographic commitment, is that you first treat each case on its own terms, almost as if it is the first case you have examined. So, the aim is first to find out what the experience of Person 2 is like, not to find out the extent to which Person 2 confirms or disconfirms what you have found for Person 1. In so doing, you should try your best to bracket what you know about the findings from the participant(s) you have already analyzed to analyze each new transcript on its own terms. Of course, this is not possible to do entirely, but it is part of the discipline of doing good IPA.

So, you take the transcript for the second interview and go through each of the steps outlined earlier for the first case (reading and initial noting, articulating experiential statements, and culminating with a single table of personal experiential themes for Case 2). Then you move to Case 3 and do the same thing again. You continue this process until you have a set of individual tables of personal experiential themes for each person in your study. You will then be ready to start comparing across cases (see Chapter 5).

5 CROSS-CASE ANALYSIS

While it is possible to write up a single case study in interpretative phenomenological analysis (IPA), most projects have a number of participants.
So, once all cases have been individually analyzed, the next stage involves
comparing across cases. We are looking to see whether there are common
patterns and idiosyncratic differences within those similarities and how one
case may shed light on another. The end result will be a new table of group
experiential themes forming the basis for writing up the analysis.

   An example is probably the easiest way to understand how to compare
across cases. Here we introduce a different study we conducted a few years
ago on the views of English women toward the issue of body organ donation. Being an organ donor means you agree that after you die, you donate
your bodily organs, such as heart, lungs, or kidney, to help improve or save
the life of someone whose organ is failing or has failed. At the time of the
interviews, England had an opt-in system, meaning an individual had to
proactively state that they wished to be on the donor register. The law has
recently changed so that individuals are now assumed to be happy with
the possibility of their organs being donated in case of their death unless
they explicitly opt out and state they do not wish to be on the register.

https://doi.org/10.1037/0000259-005
Essentials of Interpretative Phenomenological Analysis, by J. A. Smith and I. E. Nizza

At present, the United States has an opt-in system. See Exhibit 5.1 for a brief overview of the study. Part of the results have previously been published (Nizza et al., 2016).

The study had four participants, but to keep things simple, here we closely follow the themes of two of them, starting from each of their individual table of personal experiential themes through to the cross-case analysis and final table of experiential themes for the group. Exhibit 5.2 and 5.3 show the individual table of personal experiential themes for Clara and Ruth, respectively. These were our starting points, along with the tables from the two other participants. You will see the format of these tables is the same as that for Susan, our case study in the previous chapter. And indeed, they result from the same process of analysis that we described in that chapter.

The first step in a cross-case analysis is to conduct a first-pass review of each table. Each has been constructed inductively and is intended to manifest the particular lived experience of that individual. At the same time, there are likely to be overlaps between tables where participants demonstrate some similarity in their personal experiential themes. During the initial review, you look at each of the tables and see whether some reordering of personal experiential themes is warranted to facilitate the comparison process.

Thus, looking at the tables of Clara and Ruth, we can see that both demonstrate an engagement with death or mortality. In Clara's case, this appears as Personal Experiential Theme 1, but for Ruth, it is Personal Experiential Theme 2. Therefore, we moved this theme up in Ruth's table so that

---

EXHIBIT 5.1. Nondonor Thoughts and Feelings on Organ Donation

We carried out this study at a time when England had an opt-in organ donation system and people were being encouraged to register to become posthumous organ donors because only 30% of the population had done so. Also, at that time in England, in the event of suspected or imminent death, independent of somebody's registered donor status, families would be asked to decide whether their dying relative could be a donor.

We aimed to understand the experience and thinking of British women who had not registered to be donors. Four White women aged 20 to 35 (pseudonyms Jennifer, Nadine, Clara, and Ruth) were recruited. We chose a sample that would be homogenous (female, White, British, specific age group, nondonors) and easy to access. Participants were interviewed by one of two researchers, with interviews lasting between 45 and 60 minutes. What made the study particularly interesting was that, despite not having signed up to the register or discussing the matter with their families, all participants said they were in favor of organ donation.

Note. From "'You Have to Die First': Exploring the Thoughts and Feelings on Organ Donation of British Women Who Have Not Signed Up to Be Donors," by I. E. Nizza, H. P. Britton, and J. A. Smith, 2016, *Journal of Health Psychology, 21*(5), pp. 650–660 (https://doi.org/10.1177/1359105314532974). Copyright 2016 by Sage. Reprinted with permission.

EXHIBIT 5.2. Table of Personal Experiential Themes for Clara

	Page/line	Quotes
Theme 1. The problem of thinking about death		
Thought avoidance tactics	2.33	*Oh no, we won't go there.*
Death perceived as inevitable and distant	7.25	*It won't happen to me for quite a few years.*
Afterlife: possible yet unknown	3.36	*You don't know what happens after you die.*
Having jinxing thoughts	9.15	*Jinxing . . . your destiny.*
Theme 2. The difficulties of decision making		
Choice forces death to be taken into consideration	2.14	*Asking someone to kind of really take it [death] into consideration.*
Delegating decision making to others	1.29	*Assuming . . . my next of kin could give their consent.*
Considerations on the difficulty of donating one's own child	5.46	*A part of them is now with somebody else.*
Would prefer a fast process	9.8	*I'd be happy to just fill out the form and then not think about it.*
Fears of regret for not signing up	8.44	*I would hate to think that I might die and haven't registered.*
Theme 3. Feelings about self		
Being intact preserves identity	3.30	*Parts are taken away; you're not the same person.*
Mediating between rationality and irrationality	7.42	*My rational brain, then there is a part of me.*
Dislike of hesitant self	8.43	*I might be being selfish about it.*
Theme 4. Positive feelings about donation		
Possibility of saving somebody's life	4.45	*You could be saving somebody else's life.*
Donation as morally right	6.12	*I just think it is morally right.*

it became Personal Experiential Theme 1, in the same place as for Clara. The number of times this will be possible varies from project to project.

The next step in the cross-case analysis is to print out all of the tables and position them on a surface where they can be easily reviewed together in a single sweep. Your aim is to now look carefully at the material within and across cases to identify connections, similarities, and differences. Due to IPA's idiographic and inductive approach, the individual tables of personal experiential themes will inevitably be different in structure and wording. The connections you identify between them could involve similar concepts that have been worded differently or themes that appear at a higher level in one table and a lower level or as experiential statements in another.

EXHIBIT 5.3. Table of Personal Experiential Themes for Ruth

	Page/line	Quotes
Theme 1. Personal perception of the system		
Making assumptions on how system works	1.16	*I kind of assumed it would be.*
Lack of trust in the system	4.44	*Would they really know?*
Questioning the value of signing up	˙ 4.34	*It kind of feels meaningless.*
Theme 2. Difficulties considering her own mortality		
Death is difficult to talk about	9.34	*It's always a bit difficult talking about death.*
Avoiding the subject	3.15	*I would be happy to donate my organs, I suppose, if someone I loved passed away.*
Death is distant and unreal	9.41	*Who knows where we'll be by the time I actually die.*
Having alarming thoughts	5.18	*What if they put me in a coffin, and I'm not really dead?*
Powerlessness after death	7.26	*You can't speak for yourself anymore.*
Theme 3. Role of the family		
Deciding in a stressful moment	1.5	*Ask for consent when people are grieving.*
Sacrificing a loved one's body	3.19	*To chop them up seems wrong.*
Delegating her own decision	7.49	*My family would be able to speak on my behalf.*
Theme 4. The value of organs		
Value of donating brain to science	7.2	*You don't have to worry that it'll be a waste.*
Organs should not go just to anyone	6.8	*Why should I allow you to have the organs of the person I love?*

In practice, it is usually easier to begin the comparison process at the personal experiential theme level and, once some degree of synthesis is emerging, move the analysis to discrepancies at the experiential statement level. Often, finding commonalities and links requires you to move your analytical eye to a more conceptual level, where the shared higher order qualities of cases become relevant while retaining the idiosyncratic differences occurring at a more specific level between cases.

The results of your comparisons will give rise to a table of group experiential themes (sometimes called GETs), an example of which is shown in Exhibit 5.4. Here we can see how each participant is contributing to the group experiential themes and the key words that mark the evidence. Let us review this example using Clara's and Ruth's tables in Exhibit 5.2 and 5.3 to point out some of our cross-case analysis strategies.

EXHIBIT 5.4. Table of Group Experiential Themes for the Organ Donation Project

	Page/line

Group Experiential Theme 1. Attitudes to death and bodily continuity

1a. Varying ability to detach from the dead body

		Page/line
JENNIFER:	*For me it's kind of irrelevant, just my little shell.*	7.36
NADINE:	*It has been evacuated, it has gone from the vessel.*	7.27
CLARA:	*If certain parts of you are taken away, kind of, you're not the same person.*	3.30
RUTH:	*That is still a person that you've loved and to chop them up seems wrong.*	3.19-20

1b. Seeing organs as something of value

NADINE:	*If my eyes get used for somebody, or my heart.*	1.30-32
JENNIFER:	*I just think it is wasteful.*	4.35
RUTH:	*Why should I allow you to have the organs of the person I love?*	6.8

Group Experiential Theme 2. Difficult thoughts elicited by organ donation in relation to mortality

2a. Avoiding thinking about death

CLARA:	*"Oh no, we won't go there."*	2.33
JENNIFER:	*I suppose, realistically, nobody really wants to think about that.*	3.42
RUTH:	*It's always a bit difficult talking about death, isn't it?*	9.34

2b. Having irrational thoughts

NADINE:	*When I catch myself thinking it, I think "don't be an idiot."*	5.22-23
CLARA:	*Jinxing, kind of, your destiny, that occurred to me just then as well.*	9.15
RUTH:	*What if they put me in a coffin, and I'm not really dead?*	5.18

Group Experiential Theme 3. Transferring responsibility

3a. Using the family to explain not signing up

CLARA:	*Assuming . . . my next of kin could give their consent.*	1.29
RUTH:	*I think my family would be able to speak on my behalf.*	7.49
NADINE:	*Because my parents have expressed a feeling . . . I've not pursued it.*	1.45-47

3b. Using the system to explain not signing up

RUTH:	*Would they really know . . . if I ended up in hospital?*	4.44-45
CLARA:	*Perhaps it should be more of an opt-out system, that would be much easier.*	2.7
JENNIFER:	*With organ donation, I can't ever remember seeing an advert.*	2.29

Group Experiential Theme 4. Moral evaluations associated with organ donation

4a. Judgment of self for not signing up or of others for signing up

CLARA:	*I think there is a part of me that feels guilty for not signing up.*	8.42-43
JENNIFER:	*The reasons why I don't carry a card are, no, void really, it seems silly.*	3.34
NADINE:	*Well done you for actually getting your arse in gear to do it and doing it at all.*	3.33-34

4b. Positive feelings about organ donation

JENNIFER:	*The positives . . . are way too high to have any sort of negatives against it.*	4.8
NADINE:	*You might do something good for somebody without, with no effort whatsoever.*	3.29
CLARA:	*You could be saving somebody else's life.*	4.45

Group experiential themes should demonstrate a commitment to convergence and divergence. They bring together similarities in participants' accounts of their experience and so point to high-level connectivity between them. At the same time, they also point to the particular and different ways in which those participants manifest the experience. In Exhibit 5.4, let us look at Group Experiential Theme 1, "Attitudes to death and bodily continuity." All participants showed an engagement with this issue. However, as we see in Part 1a, "Varying ability to detach from the dead body," there was a stark contrast between how some participants conceptualized the body after death and how others did. As you can see from their corresponding quotes, Jennifer and Nadine described their dead bodies as a "little shell" and a "vessel," indicative of having a detached attitude. By contrast, Clara's extract "If certain parts of you are taken away, kind of, you're not the same person" suggested body integrity was key to personal identity for her. Ruth had a similar view, apparent in her quote "That is still a person that you've loved" (these can be traced back to their place in the original personal experiential themes in Exhibits 5.2 and 5.3). This theme captures how the view of the possibility of seeing a body as detached from the person is an important aspect of the attitudes expressed by participants toward organ donation.

In Exhibit 5.4, the first part of Group Experiential Theme 2 is 2a, "Avoiding thinking about death." Most participants agreed that having to think and talk about death was an obstacle to discussing organ donation within their families and elsewhere, so this was a clear area of commonality between cases. However, how this concern was manifested varied, and this can become a feature of the way the write-up is constructed.

Identifying group experiential themes is a mixture of rigorous screening across individual tables of personal experiential themes looking for links and intuitive eyeballing of the tables as a whole. The process is not a linear one; individual tables of personal experiential themes are a tool to be considered holistically. The underlying questions in the process of identifying group experiential themes are, What are the key aspects that explain what this experience is like for these people? What makes them similar to each other, and what makes them different? Here we have provided some examples to bring the process to life.

The final output is a table describing a series of group experiential themes with key words from participants to point to the evidence supporting the analysis. This is the starting point for writing up the findings from the analysis described in Chapter 6. The term "starting point" is important because, in line with IPA's iterative nature, the writing-up process itself leads to more interpretative thinking and possible restructuring of the analytic framework.

6 WRITING UP THE STUDY

You now need to write up your findings. This could be in the form of a self-contained dissertation for an undergraduate or master's degree, or it could be a journal paper or book chapter. It could also, of course, be a contribution to a doctoral thesis. Here we talk about the format for a journal article, but a similar structure operates for a bachelor's or master's degree dissertation, although the latter may be longer. We talk briefly about doctoral theses at the end of the chapter.

Journal articles reporting interpretative phenomenological analysis (IPA) studies are divided into four sections: Introduction, Method, Results, and Discussion. Due to the exploratory and inductive nature of research using IPA, the Results section is the longest and most important part of a manuscript because this is where you tell the reader what the data revealed and how you interpreted them. In consequence of what we said earlier about IPA's iterative analysis process continuing into the writing-up phase, it is common practice to write the Results section immediately at the end of the analysis to keep the momentum going and allow the interpretation to develop further. Hence, we first discuss the Results section and then, in less detail, review the contents of the other sections of a manuscript. Keep in

https://doi.org/10.1037/0000259-006
Essentials of Interpretative Phenomenological Analysis, by J. A. Smith and I. E. Nizza

mind, however, that not everybody will organize their work in this order. Some people write the Introduction and Method before the Results, and some write them before actually doing the analysis, depending on their project timeline and personal preference. Although there is no prescribed way of presenting results, there are some guidelines that we recommend you follow, particularly if it is your first time writing up an IPA study. Whichever approach is adopted, writing the manuscript, especially the Results section, will require multiple drafts and revisions, each review helping to make the arguments stronger and bringing more focus to the writing (yes, yet another iterative process!).

RESULTS SECTION

Up to this point, you will have invested a lot of effort into making sense of your data, mastering its complexity, and developing a sound structure to represent it, and you will have been working on it, probably mostly alone, in close imaginary dialogue with your participants. Now the time has come to open up that world to others: the readers of your research. While writing up the results, it is important to keep in mind that your task is to communicate your participants' world and your interpretation of how they make sense of it to others who, unlike you, have not met the participants nor read their interview transcripts nor engaged in a deep analysis of their words. To do so, you will need to tell a rich and plausible story and present the results in a narrative form that is comprehensible and compelling (Smith et al., 2009). A key facet here is the systematic alternation between the interpretation of the data and extracts from the transcript; this contributes greatly to making a narrative persuasive because the extracts give the reader a sense of what the data is like and justify the interpretation.

The Results section should start with a short summary of the findings, followed by an in-depth presentation of each group experiential theme, one at a time. The summary can be schematic, using a table or a diagram, or it can be narrative, but it needs to briefly explain what the experiential themes are and what their interrelationship is. An example of the theme summary for the organ donation project is provided in Exhibit 6.1. As you can see, it contains far less detail compared with the full group table shown in Exhibit 5.4 in the previous chapter.

In writing up each group experiential theme (or subtheme), start by including a short description of what the theme is, and then illustrate how the theme plays out for a number of participants. A standard way to do this is to take each participant in turn, introduce them, provide the relevant

EXHIBIT 6.1. Group Experiential Themes and Subthemes for the Organ Donation Project

Attitudes to death and bodily continuity
Varying ability to detach from the dead body
Seeing organs as something of value

Difficult thoughts elicited by organ donation in relation to mortality
Avoiding thinking about death
Having irrational thoughts

Transferring responsibility
Using the family to explain not signing up
Using the system to explain not signing up

Moral evaluations associated with organ donation
Judgment of self for not signing up or of others for signing up
Positive feelings about organ donation

quote from their transcript, and then offer an analytic commentary on what is happening in the extract and how it illustrates the experiential theme. Then take the next participant and do the same thing. As you go through the narrative, you will be pointing out important features that particular passages demonstrate, as well as convergences and divergences with previous extracts. One draws on enough participant quotations to indicate both the density and the breadth of the theme, and illustrators are selected for this purpose. Of course, the precise structure of the narrative will depend on the particular configuration of experiential statements, personal experiential themes, and group experiential themes that have been developed.

Exhibit 6.2 contains an example of a write-up from the first experiential subtheme of our organ donation study ("Varying ability to detach from the dead body"). You will probably remember we discussed the differing positions of the participants in relation to this issue when describing the table of group experiential themes (Chapter 5, Exhibit 5.4). Note that this write-up example is from a published article, where word count is at a premium, so the narrative is probably more concise than it would be in a dissertation. Nonetheless, it can give you a good sense of the alternation between general thematic description, participant quotes, and interpretation. To help guide you through our commentary, we have inserted numbers in the left column in Exhibit 6.2. These numbers are not part of the actual write-up and did not appear in the publication.

The section starts with an introductory paragraph describing the theme in general (1). Next, two participants are presented together (Jennifer and

EXHIBIT 6.2. Extract from Nizza, Britton, and Smith (2016)

Ability to detach from the dead body

1   All of the women seemed to assume that a person is made up of a body and a soul, but there were differences in how the moment of death was perceived: some saw death as the moment in which the body loses its function as container for the soul, while others seemed to continue to associate the body with the whole person, even after death.

2   Jennifer and Nadine described the body as holding the soul only temporarily, for as long as the person is alive. Once the person is dead, the body becomes an empty vessel or is 'evacuated' and can be made available for other practical uses such as organ donation:

3   *I think that actually, after I die, my body is kind of irrelevant, for me it's just my little shell that just holds me in place [. . .] there is nothing particularly special about the physical form as such* (Jennifer)

    What you remember of a person, what was the person [. . .] has been evacuated, it has gone from the vessel and that's all that's left, [. . .] it might as well be a side of beef (Nadine)

4   They show no feeling of attachment to the dead body, to the point that Nadine equates it to a 'side of beef', suggesting she has a very matter-of-fact and realistic approach to death. In contrast, Ruth and Clara had more difficulty at seeing death as the moment in which body and soul could separate. For Clara the most disconcerting aspect of organ donation was the potential loss of wholeness it entailed. Not knowing what lies ahead after death and being open to the possibility of an afterlife, she took what felt as a prudent view, expressing a desire to remain intact just in case the wholeness of the body could affect the wholeness of the soul, which could turn out to be a requirement for afterlife:

5   *You are somehow not the whole person, and it's kind of like, you don't know what happens after you die [laughs] and somehow wanting to remain intact or something, however irrational that is* (Clara)

6   Ruth had no doubts. For her, the dead body was definitely still the person and, at a time when the body has already been violated by death and sickness, extracting organs could extend the violation to the memory of the deceased. Her focus was on the family: the body must be preserved because that corpse is still the person they are mourning and they are not prepared to let the deceased go yet:

7   *Even if the person is a corpse, you know, at the time, that is still a person that you've loved and to kind of, chop them up, seems wrong. Seems like you're kind of, damaging their memory in some way* (Ruth)

8   In fact, Ruth found it difficult to come to terms and accept death overall, and to accept that the body should be 'chopped up' implied accepting death, which she felt unable to do:

9   *It's quite a difficult thing to accept that it's, you know, you're alive and then you're dead, and the only thing that makes you what you are is impulses in your body and biology, a scary thought* (Ruth)

EXHIBIT 6.2. Extract from Nizza, Britton, and Smith (2016) (*Continued*)

10   Interestingly, both Nadine and Jennifer described having had the experience of the death of close friends. Perhaps these experiences helped them to come to terms with the finality of death and to develop a view in which the physical body is detached from the metaphysical body. For Clara and Ruth this seemed to be more of an unresolved point. Ruth did not mention anything during the interview, but, at the end, she revealed—quite casually—that her grandmother had died the day before. This event is bound to have affected her emotionally and possibly influenced her ability to accept death, since she was probably still in a state of shock.

11   When thinking and discussing organ donation, the ability to detach the soul or identity of the dead person from the dead body would seem to be tightly connected with the ability to deeply accept the finality of death, which is a necessary condition to accept organ donation.

Note. From "'You Have to Die First': Exploring the Thoughts and Feelings on Organ Donation of British Women Who Have Not Signed Up to Be Donors," by I. E. Nizza, H. P. Britton, and J. A. Smith, 2016, *Journal of Health Psychology, 21*(5), pp. 653–654 (https://doi.org/10.1177/1359105314532974). Copyright 2016 by SAGE. Reprinted with permission.

Nadine) because they share similar feelings in relation to body and soul (2). Their view is introduced and simultaneously analyzed, followed by an illustrative quote for each of them (3) and some further interpretation (4). In the same paragraph (4), a comparison is introduced with the other two participants (Ruth and Clara), and then more details are presented regarding Clara, which are supported with a quote (5). Next, Ruth's particular position is described in two paragraphs (6 and 8), evidenced with two quotes (7 and 9). What then follows is an interpretative comparison between all four participants (10), where threads are brought together and some additional information is provided, based on things mentioned elsewhere in the interview. The final paragraph of this section (11) summarizes the overall sense of the experiential theme.

If you compare the write-up of the theme in Exhibit 6.2 with the corresponding table of group experiential themes (Exhibit 5.4 in the previous chapter), you can see that the quotes are much longer in the narrative than in the table and that in the narrative there are some quotes that were not included in the original table, such as Ruth's second quote (9). In writing up, the table of group experiential themes produced during the analysis serves as a guide; as you write, you will need to go back to the transcript to review the quotes in context, deciding exactly which quotes to use and how long they should be so that you can convey your message in the most effective way. Quotes are the means through which you bring the narrative to life, but they are also needed to ensure transparency because they allow the reader to verify how grounded in the data your claims are and to assess your overall interpretation of the data. For this reason, every time you explore a new topic within an experiential theme or as a new theme, it is important to make sure that your arguments are always supported by appropriate quotes. Quotes should always be labeled clearly using the participant pseudonyms, normally added at the end of a quote, as shown in Exhibit 6.2. This way, the reader can follow the individual journey of participants across the narrative, in accordance with the idiographic commitment of IPA researchers.

As you write up your experiential themes, one at a time, you may discover that some are richer and more meaningful than others or that the way a particular theme was broken down during the analysis is not working well in the narrative or that the order in which you are presenting the experiential themes (based on the table of themes) is not the most effective way of conveying the results of your research. This is to be expected and is not a problem because, as we have said before, writing up is part of the analysis, and the analysis is an iterative process. What is important is to be consistent throughout the manuscript; so, if a theme loses its status and is merged with another, make sure the change is reflected throughout the report (i.e., in the Method, Discussion, and abstract as well).

The results can be presented as a single continuous narrative, or they can be presented in sections, with the experiential theme titles used as headings. The choice is based on personal preference, but it is also dependent on the thematic structure: If the table contains many experiential themes, using separate sections might break up the flow too much.

In our experience, the best approach is to write the first draft quite quickly to create momentum and give a sense of the overall analysis, knowing that later you will be able to return and refine it. Your first draft may have many quite long quotes connected by limited analytic text, which can be a good starting point, particularly if you are working with IPA for the first time. During subsequent redrafting, you should aim to reverse the balance, increasing the amount of analytic narrative and making it more interpretative and shortening the quoted extracts so that they concisely illustrate the key point you are trying to convey, with no distractions. You should also consider removing quotes that do not add anything useful to the argument taking shape without forgetting that any claim you make must be grounded in the data. How many participants are in your study will also affect the structure of the narrative. For example, to make the narrative flow better, in the first paragraphs in Exhibit 6.2, Jennifer and Nadine are described together; however, to increase plausibility, there is a quote for each of them. Ruth, however, has more space, both in terms of quotes and interpretative narrative because she is the participant that best exemplifies the link between how the body is conceived and the ability to accept death (or not), which appears to be a central point in deciding whether to register as an organ donor. So, while in a single case study, by definition, the emphasis is on achieving the maximum interpretative analysis for one person, in a study with multiple participants, you need to find a balance between showing the patterning across the group, highlighting the idiographic depth of particular individuals, and giving every participant a voice.

OTHER SECTIONS OF AN IPA MANUSCRIPT

The *title* needs to convey the intrinsic nature of a study in a manner that is as succinct, informative, and captivating as possible. A title should refer to the methodology and the study findings and may include a short participant quote, if a suitable one is available, that gives voice to the phenomenon as experienced by the group as a whole. For instance, one of the studies we mentioned in Exhibit 2.1 is named "'Just Clicks': An Interpretive Phenomenological Analysis of Professional Dancers' Experience of Flow" (Hefferon & Ollis, 2006). This title encapsulates all the key aspects of the study: It is an IPA study involving professional dancers and investigating their experience of flow in their dance practice. The title also includes a short but evocative participant quote, encapsulating the essence of the experience (i.e., how flow is a psychological condition in which the mind and the body "just click," generating an optimal performance). In choosing your title, be aware that current indexing algorithms prioritize the first 60 or so characters of article titles, so it is preferable to avoid a long initial quote.

The *abstract* must summarize key information about the study to allow a potential reader to know what it is about and assess whether they should read the whole article. This latter consideration is particularly important when a study is intended for publication in an academic journal. As you may have already discovered through your literature review experience, a good abstract will save you from needlessly tracking down the full text of an article that may not be relevant to your work. The abstract should start by describing the context for the study and its aims. It should then provide key information on who the participants were, how the data were gathered (in-depth interview), how the data were analyzed (IPA), and what the findings were. A final sentence or two should summarize the overall findings and implications of the study.

The aim of the *Introduction* is to set the scene and make a case for the study. It is necessary to provide the scope and describe the research topic area, which can be done by referring to both quantitative and qualitative literature. The objective is to describe some existing work done in the field to set the context, with the aim of gradually zooming into your specific unexplored research area. In the Introduction, you should also introduce and justify IPA as the method of choice. Once the problem and the method to approach it have been defined, the Introduction may culminate with the research question.

The *Method* section must provide a step-by-step description of what conducting the research entailed. Topics to cover include how you defined and approached your sample, what information you provided before recruitment (e.g., participant information sheet), details on your actual participants, how you devised and created the interview guide, and how the interview developed in terms of consent, data recording, and transcription. The analysis process will also need to be described with a good level of detail. For student projects, this description is usually supported by examples from the project working documents (e.g., list of experiential statements, clustering process, table of personal experiential themes).

We have already discussed the Results, which is the next section in the manuscript. The purpose of the *Discussion* section is to consider the study's findings in the context of some relevant extant literature, engaging in a dialogue with existing research, and seeing what the study might be contributing. You should consider both what results are offering that is new or illuminating and, at the same time, how what has already been done by others can shed light on your findings.

IPA's inductive approach means that you will not know beforehand what results the analysis might yield. Often, results concern topics that you had not previously considered; therefore, your discussion may need to consider different or additional literature compared with what was presented in the Introduction. In such cases, you might need to do some additional selective searching through the literature to look for studies that can help you understand your novel findings and describe the context in which they could be read. Quality rather than quantity should be the criterion for choosing which literature to consider in the Discussion; ideally, you should find a few key references and use them to discuss your findings. While introducing new strands of literature in the Discussion is considered problematic in quantitative research, with IPA studies, it is normal.

In the Discussion, you will also need to evaluate your work in terms of its ability to achieve the objectives set out at the beginning and in terms of lessons you have learned in the process. A good starting point for your evaluation could be the criteria for good IPA research described by Smith (2011a,

2011b) and the American Psychological Association criteria for qualitative studies (Levitt et al., 2018), both of which are explored in Chapter 8.

The guidelines we have provided on writing the various sections of an IPA manuscript are suggestions only. You will need to adapt them to take into account the specific output for your writing (i.e., degree project report, academic journal article, or otherwise), and you might need to consider other guidelines as well. For instance, many academic institutions provide students with specific guidance on project reports, including how they should be formatted or the recommended word count. Also, make sure you consult with your academic advisor or supervisor so that your manuscript meets their expectations.

Similarly, each journal tends to have its own submission guidelines to which authors are required to adhere. Most journals have rather limited word counts, and because IPA reports tend to be lengthy, you might find yourself needing to shorten your manuscript substantially. There is no single right way to go about this, and it will depend greatly on the nature of the work you have produced. In our experience, it is often more effective to select a certain number of interrelated experiential themes to include in the paper rather than try to include a condensed version of all themes. For instance, in the article published from the organ donation study (Nizza et al., 2016), we included five of the eight experiential themes listed in Exhibit 5.4, Chapter 5.

It is more difficult to give a precise indication of the structure for a doctoral thesis. There is a great deal of flexibility and variability in how a PhD or doctorate is conducted and, therefore, written up. The thesis may contain a number of studies of different types and lengths. What is written in this chapter should be helpful in guiding you on the appropriate style for writing some of the different components of the thesis, but you should seek more specific guidance from your supervisor or advisor on the appropriate way of writing up your particular doctoral project.

Doctoral theses, which are often long, can lead to multiple articles, each focusing on a subset of the original experiential themes. The themes you choose to include in a paper submitted for publication should be able to stand alone as a cohesive whole and may be selected considering the destination journal's subject area. By focusing on fewer themes, your articles will retain the level of depth characteristic of IPA, thus hopefully increasing your chances of publication. This is definitely a case where less can be more!

7 VARIATIONS ON THE METHOD AND MORE COMPLEX DESIGNS

So far, we have talked about conducting a typical interpretative phenomenological analysis (IPA) study, in which verbal data are collected in a single interview with a small homogenous group of participants. In this chapter, we discuss some variations to the basic IPA method, such as gathering alternative types of data to combine with interviews, gathering data over time in a longitudinal design, and combining data from different people, to obtain different perspectives on a phenomenon.

The fullness of lived experience can sometimes be difficult to communicate verbally; some emotions and occurrences are so complex that finding words for them can be hard even for the most articulate participants. Visual methods are intended to help participants describe and make sense of the phenomena they experience by integrating their verbal accounts with visual representations. Some IPA researchers have begun to design studies where visual material is collected from participants alongside verbal reports. For example, to investigate the experience of chronic pain, Kirkham and colleagues (2015) asked their participants to draw their pain and then used the drawings in the interview to obtain a more in-depth and resonant account of the experience. Another example comes from Boden and colleagues (2019),

https://doi.org/10.1037/0000259-007
Essentials of Interpretative Phenomenological Analysis, by J. A. Smith and I. E. Nizza

who investigated the relational experience of their participants by asking them, during the interview, to visually "map" the relationships that were important to them. Drawings can be a powerful addition to an interview because they offer an additional entrée to prereflective insights that can accompany the more reflective verbal statements from participants. It has also been suggested that, like metaphors, the drawings can offer a "safe bridge" to express feelings that may be too difficult to express directly (Shinebourne & Smith, 2010). When included in the study report, the drawings also communicate with the viewer directly. For instance, in Kirkham et al.'s (2015) study, the pain drawings were often vivid representations of a violent aggressor or invader, conveying to the reader an almost physical sense of how difficult it is to live with chronic pain.

Photography is another visual method that has been successfully employed with IPA. Participants can be asked to take photographs of everyday objects or meaningful representations of their lives that they then discuss in the interview (Burton et al., 2017; Williamson, 2019).

In longitudinal IPA studies, researchers gather data from the same participant at a number of different time points to capture how an experience evolves over time. Longitudinal studies are usually designed around a meaningful event or experience, such as having a child, receiving a medical diagnosis, or taking part in an intervention, where you would expect time to have a significant impact on how the experience is perceived by participants. In the most effective longitudinal studies, data are gathered before and after the event or, when an event is unpredictable (e.g., bereavement), at meaningful intervals following the event (Farr & Nizza, 2019). The temporal aspect is central to this type of project, so research questions should consider the potential for change over time, and interviews should be organized at intervals that will allow change or its absence to emerge.

Longitudinal studies tend to generate large quantities of data that can be difficult and lengthy to analyze, so design decisions need to be pondered to avoid being overwhelmed by the data. Farr and Nizza (2019) conducted a review of longitudinal IPA studies and identified some key decisions researchers face: (a) how many participants to recruit initially to allow for attrition between time points, (b) whether to use the same interview guide at each time point or whether to ask different questions at different time points, and (c) whether to present the data in a way that highlights idiographic change over time or in a way that focuses on group differences over time.

Another variation on the IPA method worth mentioning here is multiperspectival studies, designed to capture more complex and systemic experiential phenomena by recruiting participants from different but usually related groups that can, as the name suggests, bring different perspectives to the understanding of the phenomena (Larkin et al., 2019). For example, the researcher might interview patients and health care providers to understand the impact of a new health intervention being offered to the patients by those health professionals. For a review of multiperspectival designs with IPA, see Larkin et al. (2019).

IPA researchers have also successfully employed focus groups to gather their data, although achieving the level of depth desirable for IPA with this method requires more researcher expertise. In focus groups, there is a dynamic between the individual and the group that can obfuscate idiographic details, particularly when the data are analyzed only at the group level. However, the same dynamic can also lead to new levels of meaning making that might not be available in a one-to-one interview (Tomkins & Eatough, 2010).

Finally, IPA is also being used in so-called mixed-methods designs, in which a qualitative and a quantitative study are combined, in sequence or in parallel, to illuminate each other's findings (Creswell & Clark, 2018). For example, IPA is used within randomized controlled trials to assess the effects of psychotherapy interventions (Wilmots et al., 2020).

As this chapter illustrates, there is a range of possible variations from a "basic" IPA design, each achieving specific objectives. Such designs are fascinating but also demanding because they entail a larger volume of data to be analyzed, more steps in the analysis, and a more layered approach to the interpretation. In general, we advise the newcomer to IPA research to stick with the more basic design. However, if you are contemplating one of these IPA design variations, we recommend that you ensure your methodological choices are well justified and that you seek inspiration from the reviews we mentioned earlier and studies that have employed the methods.

8 METHODOLOGICAL INTEGRITY

The history of evaluating the validity or quality in qualitative psychology research is an interesting one. In the early days, qualitative psychologists submitting their papers to journals for possible publication would commonly receive comments criticizing the study for failing to conform to the standards of reliability and validity developed for quantitative research. After a period of frustration at such treatment, qualitative psychologists, along with other qualitative researchers, began to develop alternative measures for assessing their work that remained truer to the basis on which qualitative research is conducted.

However, one of the tensions in early approaches was a difficulty in pitching criteria for assessment at the right level. Sometimes, evaluation instruments would be produced that tended to be overly prescriptive, offering categorical criteria often in the form of a checklist. Ironically, of course, such an approach is out of line with the relativist, interpretivist stance of most qualitative research. The other problem with some of these evaluative protocols is that, while they were intended to assist the assessment of a wide range of qualitative studies, they were framed within the perspective of one particular approach. Just as it is not appropriate to evaluate qualitative

https://doi.org/10.1037/0000259-008
Essentials of Interpretative Phenomenological Analysis, by J. A. Smith and I. E. Nizza

studies by quantitative criteria, it is not appropriate to evaluate one particular approach by criteria set up to evaluate a different approach.

What we are witnessing more recently is a welcome two-fold evolution: (a) at a macro level, the development of criteria that are genuinely pluralistic in that they are couched in terms that enable the assessment of qualitative studies from any perspective or adopting any qualitative methodology and (b) at a micro level, the development of criteria to facilitate the evaluation of studies adopting particular qualitative approaches.

We discuss two relevant papers here, each representing an example of those two mature approaches. First, we welcome the publishing of the American Psychological Association Journal Article Reporting Standards for Qualitative Research (Levitt et al., 2018), which offers a set of carefully thought through and practical recommendations to authors and reviewers in relation to the carrying out and evaluation of qualitative psychological research. The recommendations hit the right balance between specificity and generality, presenting particular items for consideration in such a way that indicates the range of ways in which those items can be addressed. We briefly outline here how a good interpretative phenomenological analysis (IPA) study, following the principles and procedures we have discussed in this book, can meet the standards outlined in that paper:

- *Introduction.* In a good IPA manuscript, researchers describe the purpose of the study, state what the central features of IPA are, and provide a rationale for employing IPA for this study.

- *Method.* Researchers describe each of the steps carried out in conducting the study: design, recruitment, data collection, analysis, and writing up. As part of that effort, a definition of purposive homogeneous sampling is provided as part of outlining the rationale for and make-up of the sample. The method of data collection is described. If this was through an in-depth interview, a short description of how the interview was conducted should be provided, along with sample questions from the interview guide.

- *Methodological integrity.* We think this is an especially strong feature of the guidelines. We concur that it is important to "demonstrate that the claims made from the analysis are warranted and have produced findings with methodological integrity" (Levitt et al., 2018, p. 36). How this is done depends on the write-up being produced. If you are writing up your dissertation for a degree, then you should be able to present considerable detail of each stage in conducting the study. This could, for example, be in the form of boxes showing annotated transcripts and thematic tables, as illustrated in Chapters 4 and 5 of this volume. For journal articles where tighter word limits are in play, of course, a more concise form of this evidence trail can be presented. However, the key thing is to state the claims you are making and how you went about substantiating them.

- *Findings and results.* In an IPA report, one needs to support claims through strong and relevant quotes from participants, followed by interpretative commentary. In line with the previous bullet point, attention should be paid to the selection of quotes to ensure, as far as possible, a proportionate representation of the corpus.

- *Discussion.* IPA researchers consider the findings in relation to the existing literature, comment on strengths and weaknesses in the study, and make suggestions for further work.

If you are doing an IPA study, we also encourage you to look at Smith's (2011a, 2011b) complementary—but more focused—guidelines that provide a set of criteria just for assessing work using IPA. The guidelines are consistent with those of Levitt et al. (2018), as described earlier, but they provide more detail on how some of these elements can be achieved in the particular way an IPA study is conducted and reported. Two other papers are also valuable resources. Smith (2011c) defined the "gem," the extract that makes a particularly outstanding and resonant contribution to the analysis, and described different types of gem that one can find in IPA writing. Nizza and colleagues (in press) presented key features to be found in good IPA papers and gave detailed illustrations from two excellent journal articles.

9 SUMMARY AND CONCLUSIONS

Interpretative phenomenological analysis (IPA) was originally developed to offer a detailed experiential qualitative methodology for psychology. While it was first adopted in psychology, it is now widely used in many disciplines—for example, management, education, health and nursing, music, and sports science. IPA has its theoretical origins in phenomenology, hermeneutics, and idiography. It is the last of these that gives IPA its most distinctive feature: a commitment to a case-study level of analysis, beginning with a detailed analysis of the first case, then doing the same with each case in turn, before looking for convergences and differences across cases. IPA is also intrinsically interpretative, and it engages with a double hermeneutic whereby the researcher is trying to make sense of the participant trying to make sense of what is happening to them. Of course, all this is to engage with the phenomenon, the lived experience of the participants being investigated in the study. The most common method for data collection in IPA is the in-depth semistructured interview, but it is also possible to collect verbal data in the form of personal accounts and diaries.

https://doi.org/10.1037/0000259-009
Essentials of Interpretative Phenomenological Analysis, by J. A. Smith and I. E. Nizza

DECIDING WHETHER IPA IS THE RIGHT METHODOLOGY FOR YOU

It is important to choose the right methodology for one's research question. There is now a clear set of qualitative methodologies available in psychology and the human and social sciences more generally, and each has a ready corpus of writings to help you with this decision. IPA is suitable for and indeed geared toward research projects concerned with examining in detail an important phenomenon of concern to the participants involved. Thus, IPA research is usually conducted on topics of experiential or even existential import. IPA is particularly valuable with research topics that are complex and ambiguous and that involve "hot cognitions," in which the participant is actively trying to make sense of an experience and the sense making is emotionally laden. We have given illustrations throughout the book of these types of research projects and research questions.

IPA's idiographic focus also means it comes into its own when one wishes to examine participants' accounts in great detail. A good IPA study offers a patterning of convergence and divergence across participants, showing with some depth both the experiential themes that the participants share and the individual way each theme is manifested for different people.

IPA offers a relatively clear set of procedures to conduct experiential qualitative research, which is particularly helpful to the newcomer who may feel intimidated by the scale of what is needed to do research in this way. At the same time, doing IPA should not be considered an easy option. The work involved at each of those described procedural steps is demanding. For those highly motivated to do such research, we expect this challenge to elicit excitement and satisfaction if sufficient effort is put into the task at hand.

Recent developments in IPA have broadened the designs that are available, as we saw in a previous chapter. Longitudinal, multimodal, and multiperspectival designs allow one to tackle another array of research questions and add to the ways in which experience can be configured and explored.

IPA is demanding both personally and in terms of the time it takes. These demands should be recognized before embarking on an IPA study. The time required to analyze each case means that sample sizes are small, and one needs to be careful in the degree of generalization one infers. However, the depth and detail of the study allow the reader to calibrate the findings and assess the degree of fit for a different group of participants.

CONCLUDING WORDS

The corpus of IPA studies is now making a major contribution to research in psychology and many other fields. Gaining a detailed insight into the patterning of similarities and differences in how participants describe and make sense of significant things they are experiencing offers an important and distinctive lens on these phenomena. It is also the case that the accumulating corpus of IPA research enables the development of metasyntheses that can make claims to a much broader population.

Such individual IPA studies are important in their own right in offering detailed examinations of personal lived experience. However, they can also contribute in other ways. IPA studies can help illuminate questions that arise from prior quantitative studies in the area. They can also inform interventions to help alleviate psychological and social problems. IPA can also be used alongside quantitative methods in sophisticated mixed-methods studies on complex issues. Have a look at the list of good IPA studies we present in the Appendix to see just a small sample of the different ways IPA is beginning to make an important contribution to knowledge.

We hope you have found reading this book interesting and stimulating. If you are doing an IPA study or intend to, we hope the book helps you with the process. If you have a more general interest in qualitative methodology, we hope the book has helped you get a clearer understanding of IPA's origins and processes. If you want to find out more about IPA, we suggest you look at *Interpretative Phenomenological Analysis: Theory, Method and Research* by Smith and colleagues (2009), which has more detail on, for example, its theoretical underpinnings and connections with other approaches and also includes good examples of it in practice. A useful IPA website, http://www.ipa.bbk.ac.uk/, documents, for example, upcoming events, useful reading, and regional and international IPA interest groups.

Appendix

EXEMPLAR STUDIES

Bramley, N., & Eatough, V. (2005). The experience of living with Parkinson's disease: An interpretative phenomenological analysis case study. *Psychology & Health, 20*(2), 223–235. https://doi.org/10.1080/08870440412331296053

Conroy, D., & de Visser, R. (2015). The importance of authenticity for student non-drinkers: An interpretative phenomenological analysis. *Journal of Health Psychology, 20*(11), 1483–1493. https://doi.org/10.1177/1359105313514285

Dickson, A., Knussen, C., & Flowers, P. (2008). 'That was my old life; it's almost like a past-life now': Identity crisis, loss and adjustment amongst people living with Chronic Fatigue Syndrome. *Psychology & Health, 23*(4), 459–476. https://doi.org/10.1080/08870440701757393

Dwyer, A., Heary, C., Ward, M., & MacNeela, P. (2019). Adding insult to brain injury: Young adults' experiences of residing in nursing homes following acquired brain injury. *Disability and Rehabilitation, 41*(1), 33–43. https://doi.org/10.1080/09638288.2017.1370732

Holland, F. G., Peterson, K., & Archer, S. (2018). Thresholds of size: An interpretative phenomenological analysis of childhood messages around food, body, health and weight. *Journal of Critical Dietetics, 4*(1), 25–36.

Huff, J. L., Smith, J. A., Jesiek, B. K., Zoltowski, C. B., & Oakes, W. C. (2019). Identity in engineering adulthood: An interpretative phenomenological analysis of early-career engineers in the United States as they transition to the workplace. *Emerging Adulthood, 7*(6), 451–467. https://doi.org/10.1177/2167696818780444

McDonough, M. H., Sabiston, C. M., & Ullrich-French, S. (2011). The development of social relationships, social support, and posttraumatic growth in a dragon boating team for breast cancer survivors. *Journal of Sport and Exercise Psychology, 33*(5), 627–648. https://doi.org/10.1123/jsep.33.5.627

Nizza, I. E., Smith, J. A., & Kirkham, J. A. (2018). 'Put the illness in a box': A longitudinal interpretative phenomenological analysis of changes in a sufferer's pictorial representations of pain following participation in a pain management programme. *British Journal of Pain, 12*(3), 163–170. https://doi.org/10.1177/2049463717738804

Oakland, J., MacDonald, R., & Flowers, P. (2013). Identity in crisis: The role of work in the formation and renegotiation of a musical identity. *British Journal of Music Education, 30*(2), 261–276. https://doi.org/10.1017/S026505171300003X

Rostill-Brookes, H., Larkin, M., Toms, A., & Churchman, C. (2011). A shared experience of fragmentation: Making sense of foster placement breakdown. *Clinical Child Psychology and Psychiatry, 16*(1), 103–127. https://doi.org/10.1177/1359104509352894

Smith, J. A., & Rhodes, J. E. (2015). Being depleted and being shaken: An interpretative phenomenological analysis of the experiential features of a first episode of depression. *Psychology and Psychotherapy: Theory, Research and Practice, 88*(2), 197–209. https://doi.org/10.1111/papt.12034

Spiers, J., Smith, J. A., & Drage, M. (2015). A longitudinal interpretative phenomenological analysis of the process of kidney recipients' resolution of complex ambiguities within relationships with their living donors. *Journal of Health Psychology, 21*(11), 2600–2611. https://doi.org/10.1177/1359105315581070

References

Ashworth, P. D. (2015). Conceptual foundations of qualitative psychology. In J. A. Smith (Ed.), *Qualitative psychology: A practical guide to research methods* (3rd ed., pp. 4–24). SAGE.

Boden, Z., Larkin, M., & Iyer, M. (2019). Picturing ourselves in the world: Drawings, interpretative phenomenological analysis and the relational mapping interview. *Qualitative Research in Psychology, 16*(2), 218–236. https://doi.org/10.1080/14780887.2018.1540679

Brinkman, S., & Kvale, S. (2015). *Interviews: Learning the craft of qualitative research interviewing* (3rd ed.). SAGE.

Bromley, D. B. (1986). *The case-study method in psychology and related disciplines.* Wiley.

Burr, V. (2006). *An introduction to social constructionism.* Routledge. https://doi.org/10.4324/9780203133026

Burton, A., Hughes, M., & Dempsey, R. C. (2017). Quality of life research: A case for combining photo-elicitation with interpretative phenomenological analysis. *Qualitative Research in Psychology, 14*(4), 375–393. https://doi.org/10.1080/14780887.2017.1322650

Churchill, S. D. (2022). *Essentials of existential phenomenological research.* American Psychological Association. https://doi.org/10.1037/0000257-000

Creswell, J. W., & Clark, V. L. P. (2018). *Designing and conducting mixed methods research* (3rd ed.). SAGE.

Farr, J., & Nizza, I. E. (2019). Longitudinal interpretative phenomenological analysis (LIPA): A review of studies and methodological considerations. *Qualitative Research in Psychology, 16*(2), 199–217. https://doi.org/10.1080/14780887.2018.1540677

Finlay, L. (2009). Ambiguous encounters: A relational approach to phenomenological research. *The Indo-Pacific Journal of Phenomenology, 9*(1), 1–17. https://doi.org/10.1080/20797222.2009.11433983

Giorgi, A. (1997). The theory, practice, and evaluation of the phenomenologi-cal method as a qualitative research procedure. *Journal of Phenomenological Psychology, 28*(2), 235–260. https://doi.org/10.1163/156916297X00103

Halling, S. (2008). *Intimacy, transcendence, and psychology: Closeness and openness in everyday life.* Palgrave. https://doi.org/10.1057/9780230610255

Hefferon, K. M., & Ollis, S. (2006). 'Just clicks': An interpretive phenomenolog-ical analysis of professional dancers' experience of flow. *Research in Dance Education, 7*(2), 141–159. https://doi.org/10.1080/14647890601029527

Heidegger, M. (1962). *Being and time.* Blackwell. (Original work published 1927)

Hepburn, A., & Potter, J. (2021). *Essentials of conversation analysis.* American Psychological Association.

Husserl, E. (2001). *Logical investigations* (Vol. 1). Routledge. (Original work pub-lished 1900)

Kirkham, J. A., Smith, J. A., & Havsteen-Franklin, D. (2015). Painting pain: An interpretative phenomenological analysis of representations of living with chronic pain. *Health Psychology, 34*(4), 398–406. https://doi.org/10.1037/hea0000139

Lamiell, J. T. (1987). *The psychology of personality: An epistemological inquiry.* Columbia University Press.

Larkin, M., Eatough, V., & Osborn, M. (2011). Interpretative phenomenological analysis and embodied, active, situated cognition. *Theory & Psychology, 21*(3), 318–337. https://doi.org/10.1177/0959354310377544

Larkin, M., Shaw, R., & Flowers, P. (2019). Multiperspectival designs and processes in interpretative phenomenological analysis research. *Qualitative Research in Psychology, 16*(2), 182–198. https://doi.org/10.1080/14780887.2018.1540655

Larkin, M., Watts, S., & Clifton, E. (2006). Giving voice and making sense in inter-pretative phenomenological analysis. *Qualitative Research in Psychology, 3*(2), 102–120. https://doi.org/10.1191/1478088706qp062oa

Levitt, H. M., Bamberg, M., Creswell, J. W., Frost, D. M., Josselson, R., & Suárez-Orozco, C. (2018). Journal article reporting standards for qualitative primary, qualitative meta-analytic, and mixed methods research in psychology: The APA Publications and Communications Board task force report. *American Psycholo-gist, 73*(1), 26–46. https://doi.org/10.1037/amp0000151

McDonough, M. H., Sabiston, C. M., & Ullrich-French, S. (2011). The development of social relationships, social support, and posttraumatic growth in a dragon boating team for breast cancer survivors. *Journal of Sport & Exercise Psychology, 33*(5), 627–648. https://doi.org/10.1123/jsep.33.5.627

McMullen, L. (2021). *Essentials of discursive psychology.* American Psychological Association. https://doi.org/10.1037/0000220-000

Nizza, I. E., Britton, H. P., & Smith, J. A. (2016). 'You have to die first': Exploring the thoughts and feelings on organ donation of British women who have not signed up to be donors. *Journal of Health Psychology, 21*(5), 650–660. https://doi.org/10.1177/1359105314532974

Nizza, I. E., Farr, J., & Smith, J. A. (in press). Achieving excellence in interpretative phenomenological analysis (IPA) studies: Four markers of high quality. *Qualitative Research in Psychology*.

Platt, J. (1988). What can case studies do? In R. G. Burgess (Ed.), *Studies in qualitative methodology* (pp. 1–23). JAI Press.

Reicher, S. (2000). Against methodolatry: Some comments. on Elliott, Fischer, and Rennie. *British Journal of Clinical Psychology*, *39*(1), 1–6. https://doi.org/10.1348/014466500163031

Rostill-Brookes, H., Larkin, M., Toms, A., & Churchman, C. (2011). A shared experience of fragmentation: Making sense of foster placement breakdown. *Clinical Child Psychology and Psychiatry*, *16*(1), 103–127. https://doi.org/10.1177/1359104509352894

Shinebourne, P., & Smith, J. A. (2010). The communicative power of metaphors: An analysis and interpretation of metaphors in accounts of the experience of addiction. *Psychology and Psychotherapy: Theory, Research and Practice*, *83*(1), 59–73. https://doi.org/10.1348/147608309X468077

Smith, J. A. (1996). Beyond the divide between cognition and discourse: Using interpretative phenomenological analysis in health psychology. *Psychology & Health*, *11*(2), 261–271. https://doi.org/10.1080/08870449608400256

Smith, J. A. (1999). Identity development during the transition to motherhood: An interpretative phenomenological analysis. *Journal of Reproductive and Infant Psychology*, *17*(3), 281–299. https://doi.org/10.1080/02646839908404595

Smith, J. A. (2007). Hermeneutics, human sciences and health: Linking theory and practice. *International Journal of Qualitative Studies on Health and Wellbeing*, *2*(1), 3–11. https://doi.org/10.1080/17482620601016120

Smith, J. A. (2011a). Evaluating the contribution of interpretative phenomenological analysis. *Health Psychology Review*, *5*(1), 9–27. https://doi.org/10.1080/17437199.2010.510659

Smith, J. A. (2011b). Evaluating the contribution of interpretative phenomenological analysis: A reply to the commentaries and further development of criteria. *Health Psychology Review*, *5*(1), 55–61. https://doi.org/10.1080/17437199.2010.541743

Smith, J. A. (2011c). "We could be diving for pearls": The value of the gem in experiential qualitative psychology. *Qualitative Methods in Psychology Bulletin*, *12*, 6–15.

Smith, J. A. (2019). Participants and researchers searching for meaning: Conceptual developments for interpretative phenomenological analysis. *Qualitative Research in Psychology*, *16*(2), 166–181. https://doi.org/10.1080/14780887.2018.1540648

Smith, J. A., Flowers, P., & Larkin, M. (2009). *Interpretative phenomenological analysis: Theory, method and research*. SAGE.

Smith, J. A., Harré, R., & Van Langenhove, L. (1995). Idiography and the case study. In J. A. Smith, R. Harré, & L. Van Langenhove (Eds.), *Rethinking methods in psychology* (pp. 57–69). SAGE.

Smith, J. A., & Osborn, M. (2003). Interpretative phenomenological analysis. In J. A. Smith (Ed.), *Qualitative psychology* (pp. 51–80). SAGE.

Todres, L., Galvin, K., & Dahlberg, K. (2007). Lifeworld-led healthcare: Revisiting a humanising philosophy that integrates emerging trends. *Medicine, Health Care, and Philosophy, 10*(1), 53–63. https://doi.org/10.1007/s11019-006-9012-8

Tomkins, L., & Eatough, V. (2010). Reflecting on the use of IPA with focus groups: Pitfalls and potentials. *Qualitative Research in Psychology, 7*(3), 244–262. https://doi.org/10.1080/14780880903121491

Van Manen, M. (2016). *Researching lived experience: Human science for an action sensitive pedagogy.* Routledge.

Williamson, I. (2019). 'I am everything but myself': Exploring visual voice accounts of single mothers caring for a daughter with Rett syndrome. *Qualitative Research in Psychology, 16*(4), 566–590. https://doi.org/10.1080/14780887.2018.1431751

Wilmots, E., Midgley, N., Thackeray, L., Reynolds, S., & Loades, M. (2020). The therapeutic relationship in Cognitive Behaviour Therapy with depressed adolescents: A qualitative study of good-outcome cases. *Psychology and Psychotherapy: Theory, Research and Practice, 93*(2), 276–291. https://doi.org/10.1111/papt.12232

Index

Title
  of personal experiential theme, 46
  of study, 63
Tone of voice, 27
Topics, research, 3, 11–13, 63. *See also*
    Sensitive topics
Transcripts, interview
  checking, 16
  creating, 27–30
  exploratory notes on, 32–38
  reading, 32–33
Traveling solo case example
  clustering experiential statements in,
      43–45, 47–49
  conducting interviews in, 23–26
  experiential statements for, 39–42
  exploratory notes for, 33–38
  interview guide for, 21
  research design for, 18
  table of personal experiential themes
      from, 45–46
  transcript for, 27–29
Trust building, 24

U

Undergraduate research projects, 15–16, 65

V

Validity, 71
Verbal data, in IPA studies, 67
Virtual interviewing, 14
Visual methods, IPA with, 67–68

W

Well-being
  participant, 17
  researcher, 18
Word counts, journal article, 65
Writing up studies, 57–65
  cross-case analysis as starting point for,
      56
  guidelines for, 63–65
  in Results section, 58–63
  time commitment for, 16

About the Authors

Jonathan A. Smith, DPhil, is a professor of psychology at Birkbeck University of London, United Kingdom, where he leads the Interpretative Phenomenological Analysis (IPA) Research Group and teaches qualitative methods at all levels. Previously, he held academic positions at the Universities of Keele and Sheffield after completing his doctorate at the University of Oxford. He developed IPA as a particular experiential qualitative approach in psychology, and he has applied it to a wide range of research questions, many in health and illness. He was elected an Honorary Fellow of the British Psychological Society in 2020.

Isabella E. Nizza is a qualitative researcher who specializes in researching the lived experience of chronic health conditions using IPA. For many years a corporate trainer and consultant, she is now part of the Interpretative Phenomenological Analysis Research Group within the Department of Psychological Sciences at Birkbeck University of London, where she also teaches qualitative methods. At the moment, she is working on a randomized controlled trial testing a psychological support intervention for young people with epilepsy, using IPA to assess the intervention's psychological outcomes and process.

About the Series Editors

Clara E. Hill, PhD, earned her doctorate at Southern Illinois University in 1974. She started her career in 1974 as an assistant professor in the Department of Psychology, University of Maryland, College Park, and is currently there as a professor.

She is the president-elect of the Society for the Advancement of Psychotherapy, and has been the president of the Society for Psychotherapy Research, the editor of the *Journal of Counseling Psychology*, and the editor of *Psychotherapy Research*.

Dr. Hill was awarded the Leona Tyler Award for Lifetime Achievement in Counseling Psychology from Division 17 (Society of Counseling Psychology) and the Distinguished Psychologist Award from Division 29 (Society for the Advancement of Psychotherapy) of the American Psychological Association, the Distinguished Research Career Award from the Society for Psychotherapy Research, and the Outstanding Lifetime Achievement Award from the Section on Counseling and Psychotherapy Process and Outcome Research of the Society of Counseling Psychology. Her major research interests are helping skills, psychotherapy process and outcome, training therapists, dream work, and qualitative research.

She has published more than 250 journal articles, 80 chapters in books, and 17 books (including *Therapist Techniques and Client Outcomes: Eight Cases of Brief Psychotherapy*; *Helping Skills: Facilitating Exploration, Insight, and Action*; and *Dream Work in Therapy: Facilitating Exploration, Insight, and Action*).

Sarah Knox, PhD, joined the faculty of Marquette University in 1999 and is a professor in the Department of Counselor Education and Counseling Psychology in the College of Education. She earned her doctorate at the

University of Maryland and completed her predoctoral internship at The Ohio State University.

Dr. Knox's research has been published in a number of journals, including *The Counseling Psychologist, Counselling Psychology Quarterly, Journal of Counseling Psychology, Psychotherapy, Psychotherapy Research,* and *Training and Education in Professional Psychology.* Her publications focus on the psychotherapy process and relationship, supervision and training, and qualitative research. She has presented her research both nationally and internationally and has provided workshops on consensual qualitative research at both U.S. and international venues.

She currently serves as coeditor-in-chief of *Counselling Psychology Quarterly* and is also on the publication board of Division 29 (Society for the Advancement of Psychotherapy) of the American Psychological Association. Dr. Knox is a fellow of Division 17 (Society of Counseling Psychology) and Division 29 of the American Psychological Association.